Chicago Top 40 Charts
1970-1979

Chicago Top 40 Charts
1970-1979

Compiled by Ron Smith

Writers Club Press
San Jose   New York   Lincoln   Shanghai

Chicago Top 40 Charts 1970-1979

Writers Club Press
an imprint of iUniverse, Inc.

For information address:
iUniverse, Inc.
5220 S. 16th St., Suite 200
Lincoln, NE 68512
www.iuniverse.com

ISBN: 0-595-20622-0

Printed in the United States of America

To Jackie, the inspiration for everything good I do in my life.

CONTENTS

ACKNOWLEDGEMENTS

Thank you to those who inspired or helped in compiling this book: Dick Biondi, John Charleson, Dave Douglas, J.R. Dykema, Tommy Edwards, Scott Fischer, Jim Furholmen, Bill Ganson, Barbara Jastrab, Randy Lane, Jack Miller, Lorna Ozmon, Art Roberts, Kurt Scholle, Jim Smith and Bill Stedman. A special thanks to the person who inspires every book of this type, Joel Whitburn.

INTRODUCTION

In *Chicago Top 40 Charts 1970-1979*, we continue our journey through the Windy City's top hits as documented by the weekly record store surveys issued by radio station WLS.

As rock 'n' roll music entered its third decade, it was finding itself increasingly fragmented. Progressive and album rock, oldies and adult contemporary stations all combined to shatter the ratings dominance top 40 radio had exhibited throughout the 1960s. But while FM listening overtook AM in the rest of the country by the decade's end, Chicago was the exception. WLS managed to stave off its competition (including perennial nemesis WCFL, who changed formats to beautiful music in 1976) with memorable promotions and the strongest air personalities available. And what never changed was their commitment to playing Chicago's favorite music—regardless of genre.

As evidence, all we have to do is look at the top tunes on WLS in May of 1974. They included a topical novelty record (Ray Stevens' "The Streak"); a pop version of "The Lord's Prayer" by Australian nun Sister Janet Mead; a Scott Joplin ragtime tune written in 1902 ("The Entertainer" from Marvin Hamlisch); two remakes—one a hard rock version of a classic oldie (Grand Funk's "Loco-Motion"), the other a goofy Swedish import ("Hooked On A Feeling" by Blue Swede); quintessential Philadelphia soul ("TSOP" from MFSB); a posthumous hit for Jim Croce ("I'll Have To Say I Love You In A Song") and the latest from the decade's top artist, Elton John ("Bennie And The Jets"). Such variety would stagger the mind of today's contemporary hit radio listener.

On the surface, the WLS surveys in the 1970s seem very conservative. At one point, only 20 songs are listed on the chart. Local groups (except for supergroup Chicago) show up infrequently at best. But there are flashes of the independence that the station was known for in the previous decade: a one-hit wonder group from Canada named Wednesday tops the WLS chart with their version of J. Frank Wilson's "Last Kiss", the Beatles make their final appearance atop the charts with "Got To Get You Into My Life" and WLS starts playing an old Styx tune named "Lady" so much that the group's label is forced to re-release it, launching the local band on their way to superstardom.

As in the first volume in this series, *Chicago Top 40 Charts 1970-1979* lists every song to reach the WLS survey (by this time the "Silver Dollar Survey" moniker had long since been dropped) alphabetically by title and artist, with debut and peak dates, highest position reached and number of weeks on the charts. The top songs of each year and for the entire decade are ranked as well. As an added bonus, this volume features the "Big 89 Artists of the 1970s", a list which should surprise many people.

Chicago Top 40 Charts 1970-1979 was made possible by the outpouring of support shown for my 1960s chart book. Thank you, all. And as for the 1980s? Just as before, the success of this book should enable its release.

METHODOLOGY

This book is a continuation of *Chicago Top 40 Charts 1960-1969* and covers every tune that charted on the WLS weekly music survey from January 5, 1970 through December 29, 1979.

As in the first book, **Debut** is the date the song first appears on the charts. **Peak** is the date it first reaches its highest position. **Pos** is the highest position reached on the charts and **Wks** is the number of weeks it appears on the charts.

On two occasions, special year-end charts took the place of the normal survey. As in the first book in this series, songs that appeared on the charts before and after the special survey are given credit for the missing week. Songs debuting after the special survey are not credited for the previous week, even when their debut position is rather high. Songs that drop off the chart after a special survey are not credited for the missing week. During any missing weeks, all songs not appearing are considered "frozen" at their previous position but are given credit for the week on the chart.

At times, "two-sided hits" appeared on the charts. Both the "A" and "B" sides of a record would be listed. Any time both sides were listed, the "B" side also received credit for the position reached and that week on the chart. However, often the "B" side was only listed during part of the record's run on the chart. Only the weeks a "B" side was actually listed is credited. Therefore, while Donny Osmond's "A Million To One" receives the same chart credit as its "A" side, "Young Love", because both songs were listed every week; "Fool" by Elvis Presley receives credit for four less weeks and one lower position than its "A" side, "Steamroller Blues", because it was only listed one-third of the time. In the artist listing, "B" sides are preceded by a slash and listed under their "A" sides.

Artists often recorded under different variations of their names. Name variations are indented under the original artist name. Totally different groups or names are listed separately, with a notation to "also see" the other artist.

The size of the charts varied in the seventies, presenting a challenge in compiling this book. In mid-1970, the survey changed from 40 to 30 songs, usually with one or two "Hit Parade Bound" extras. In March of 1972, the printed survey was abandoned altogether, in favor of giant posters sent to record stores with the "Big 8 and 9" songs plus as many as 16 extras. By July of 1973, the printed surveys were back with a fixed 30 songs that expanded to 40 again later that year. But by February of the next year, an evolution occurred that took the survey from 40 down to 15 tunes with a varying number of extras (from 3 to 15). In December of 1975, the most dramatic change of all occurred. The list expanded to 45 songs, sometimes with as many as four extras. Up until that date, WLS had played all of the songs on the list. From this point forward, the survey represented the top songs in Chicago regardless of whether WLS was playing them.

Since the extra songs on each incarnation of the survey are in rank order, credit was given to them as if numbering continued. So the six extra songs listed on the July 20, 1974 survey were credited here as #16 through #21. This causes a dilemma, however, on at least two occasions when the surveys expand. Using the methodology just described, "Rhinestone Cowboy" by Glen Campbell should be given credit for being the #30 song on the December 20, 1975 survey. However, when the list expands from 15 songs with extras to 45 songs the following week, WLS says it was #32 "last week". This is because there were two songs the station wasn't playing ("Venus & Mars Rock Show" by Wings and "Last Game Of The Season" by David Geddes) that it didn't list previously but now did. Because *Chicago Top 40 Charts 1970-1979* is a compilation of the public (printed) WLS surveys and not any internal station lists, I have chosen to ignore such anomalies. Glen Campbell, therefore is credited with #30 for the disputed week.

There was some confusion in the first book concerning the yearly top 40 lists. They are not the printed WLS year-end lists, because in the early years the station did not issue such a countdown. I chose therefore, to create my own objective ranking of the year's (and decade's) top songs, based on highest position reached, weeks at that highest position, weeks on the chart, followed by weeks in the top ten, twenty and top five, in that order. That practice is continued in this book.

Finally, the top artists of the decade is based simply on points awarded based on highest position reached for every charted song by an artist with bonus points for each week on the chart.

ALPHABETICAL LISTING BY ARTIST

Artist	Title	Debut	Peak	Pos	Wks
ABBA					
	Waterloo	6/29/74	7/27/74	3	11
	SOS	10/25/75	11/22/75	6	16
	Fernando	9/18/76	10/23/76	14	11
	Dancing Queen	2/5/77	4/9/77	1	20
	Knowing Me, Knowing You	6/4/77	8/13/77	5	19
	Take A Chance On Me	6/17/78	8/5/78	7	17
	Does Your Mother Know	7/21/79	8/18/79	28	11
Ace					
	How Long	4/12/75	5/10/75	8	15
Addrisi Brothers					
	Slow Dancin' Don't Turn Me On	6/11/77	7/16/77	31	8
Aerosmith					
	Dream On	2/7/76	3/20/76	2	18
	Walk This Way	12/18/76	1/29/77	4	15
Albert, Morris					
	Feelings	11/15/75	12/13/75	1	18
Alive and Kicking					
	Tighter, Tighter	6/22/70	8/3/70	3	12
Allman, Gregg					
	Midnight Rider	12/29/73	2/2/74	18	8
Allman Brothers Band					
	Ramblin Man	9/8/73	10/13/73	3	13
Alpert, Herb					
	Rise	9/8/79	10/27/79	1	23
Amazing Rhythm Aces					
	Third Rate Romance	10/4/75	10/11/75	12	3

Artist Title	Debut	Peak	Pos	Wks
Ambrosia				
How Much I Feel	11/4/78	12/9/78	8	17
America				
A Horse With No Name	3/6/72	3/27/72	1	11
I Need You	5/29/72	7/3/72	7	7
Ventura Highway	10/30/72	12/11/72	6	11
Tin Man	10/26/74	12/7/74	4	14
Lonely People	2/8/75	3/22/75	5	14
Sister Golden Hair	5/10/75	6/21/75	1	18
Today's The Day	6/5/76	7/24/76	25	11
Anderson, Lynn				
Rose Garden	1/4/71	1/18/71	23	3
Anka, Paul with Odia Coates				
(You're) Having My Baby	8/17/74	9/7/74	1	14
One Man Woman/One Woman Man	12/14/74	12/28/74	10	6
I Don't Like To Sleep Alone	5/10/75	5/24/75	12	3
Anka, Paul				
Times Of Your Life	1/3/76	2/21/76	35	9
Apollo 100				
Joy	1/31/72	2/21/72	4	11
April Wine				
You Could Have Been A Lady	4/24/72	5/22/72	14	7
Archies				
Jingle Jangle	12/1/69	1/5/70	8	9
Who's Your Baby	3/2/70	4/6/70	22	6
Sunshine	7/20/70	8/3/70	26	3
Argent				
Hold Your Head Up	7/17/72	8/28/72	4	10
Ashton, Gardner & Dyke				
Resurrection Shuffle	7/19/71	8/30/71	5	11
Assembled Multitude				
Overture From Tommy (A Rock Opera)	8/17/70	8/31/70	19	4

Artist	Title	Debut	Peak	Pos	Wks
Atlanta Rhythm Section					
	So In To You	2/19/77	4/9/77	8	18
	Imaginary Lover	4/29/78	6/17/78	9	17
	Do It Or Die	7/7/79	8/4/79	19	11
	Spooky	11/3/79	11/24/79	32	7
Average White Band					
	Pick Up The Pieces	3/1/75	3/22/75	12	5
Babys					
	Isn't It Time	11/5/77	12/17/77	8	16
	Every Time I Think Of You	3/17/79	4/14/79	20	12
Bachman-Turner Overdrive					
	Takin' Care Of Business	7/13/74	8/17/74	2	12
	You Ain't Seen Nothing Yet	10/19/74	11/16/74	1	16
	Roll On Down The Highway	1/25/75	3/8/75	4	15
	Hey You	6/21/75	7/12/75	9	7
	also see the Guess Who				
Bad Company					
	Can't Get Enough	10/5/74	11/2/74	6	12
	Feel Like Makin' Love	10/4/75	10/18/75	7	4
	Rock 'N' Roll Fantasy	6/2/79	8/4/79	9	19
	also see Free				
Badfinger					
	Come And Get It	2/23/70	4/6/70	3	11
	No Matter What	11/30/70	12/21/70	6	6
	Day After Day	12/13/71	1/17/72	2	14
	Baby Blue	4/3/72	5/1/72	2	10
Baez, Joan					
	The Night They Drove Old Dixie Down	8/16/71	9/20/71	2	11
	Let It Be	11/29/71	12/13/71	17	4

Artist	Title	Debut	Peak	Pos	Wks
Baker, George, Selection					
	Little Green Bag	3/30/70	5/18/70	4	12
	Paloma Blanca	1/31/76	2/21/76	32	10
Band					
	Up On Cripple Creek	11/10/69	12/15/69	11	10
Bar-Kays					
	Shake Your Rump To The Funk	11/20/76	11/27/76	42	4
Barron Knights					
	The Topical Song	8/25/79	9/22/79	29	9
Bay City Rollers					
	Saturday Night	11/29/75	12/20/75	1	25
	Money Honey	2/21/76	3/20/76	7	14
	Rock And Roll Love Letter	5/8/76	6/26/76	4	15
	I Only Want To Be With You	9/4/76	10/30/76	2	23
	Yesterday's Hero	1/1/77	1/29/77	20	8
	Dedication	3/12/77	3/26/77	38	4
	You Made Me Believe In Magic	6/18/77	7/30/77	2	17
	The Way I Feel Tonight	12/17/77	1/28/78	19	11
Bazuka					
	Dynamite—Part I	8/2/75	8/23/75	8	6
Beach Boys					
	Add Some Music To Your Day	3/9/70	3/9/70	39	2
	Rock And Roll Music	6/5/76	7/31/76	2	19
	It's O.K.	9/4/76	10/2/76	23	7
Beatles					
	Come Together	10/6/69	11/3/69	1	16
	/Something	10/6/69	11/3/69	1	16
	Let It Be	3/9/70	3/30/70	1	10
	The Long And Winding Road	5/18/70	6/22/70	1	13
	Got To Get You Into My Life	6/5/76	7/10/76	1	17
	Ob-La-Di, Ob-La-Da	11/27/76	12/11/76	33	5

also see Lennon, John; McCartney, Paul; Harrison, George & Starr, Ringo

Artist	Title	Debut	Peak	Pos	Wks

Bee Gees

Title	Debut	Peak	Pos	Wks
Lonely Days	12/14/70	1/4/71	2	9
How Can You Mend A Broken Heart	6/28/71	8/2/71	1	10
Don't Wanna Live Inside Myself	10/25/71	11/8/71	18	4
My World	2/7/72	2/28/72	9	9
Run To Me	8/28/72	9/18/72	14	7
Jive Talkin'	7/26/75	8/23/75	2	17
Nights On Broadway	11/15/75	12/6/75	7	15
Fanny (Be Tender With My Love)	1/10/76	2/21/76	9	17
You Should Be Dancing	7/24/76	9/4/76	5	17
Love So Right	10/2/76	11/27/76	14	14
Boogie Child	2/12/77	3/12/77	23	7
How Deep Is Your Love	10/29/77	12/24/77	1	31
Stayin' Alive	1/7/78	2/11/78	1	31
Night Fever	2/25/78	5/6/78	1	26
Too Much Heaven	12/2/78	2/3/79	3	23
Tragedy	2/17/79	4/7/79	4	20
Love You Inside Out	5/12/79	6/16/79	9	14

Beginning Of The End

Title	Debut	Peak	Pos	Wks
Funky Nassau—Part I	6/14/71	7/19/71	9	7

Bell, Benny

Title	Debut	Peak	Pos	Wks
Shaving Cream	3/22/75	4/26/75	12	8

Bell, Vincent

Title	Debut	Peak	Pos	Wks
Airport Love Theme (Gwen And Vern)	4/6/70	5/18/70	16	11

Bell, William

Title	Debut	Peak	Pos	Wks
Tryin' To Love Two	3/26/77	4/30/77	25	9

Bell & James

Title	Debut	Peak	Pos	Wks
Livin' It Up (Friday Night)	2/24/79	3/24/79	24	13

Bellamy Brothers

Title	Debut	Peak	Pos	Wks
Let Your Love Flow	3/27/76	5/15/76	3	17

Belle Epoque

Title	Debut	Peak	Pos	Wks
Miss Broadway	2/25/78	4/8/78	27	14

Bells

Title	Debut	Peak	Pos	Wks
Stay Awhile	4/5/71	4/26/71	6	8

Artist Title	Debut	Peak	Pos	Wks
Benson, George				
This Masquerade	7/17/76	8/28/76	15	12
On Broadway	4/29/78	6/10/78	13	17
Love Ballad	4/28/79	5/26/79	26	8
Benton, Brook				
Rainy Night In Georgia	1/26/70	3/16/70	4	12
Bishop, Elvin				
Fooled Around And Fell In Love	4/17/76	6/19/76	4	15
Bishop, Stephen				
On And On	8/13/77	10/29/77	8	19
Black Oak Arkansas				
Jim Dandy	1/12/74	3/9/74	9	10
Blanchard, Jack & Misty Morgan				
Tennessee Bird Walk	3/16/70	4/13/70	12	8
Blondie				
Heart Of Glass	3/31/79	6/2/79	2	26
One Way Or Another	8/18/79	9/22/79	31	15
Dreaming	11/24/79	12/15/79	23	12
Blood, Sweat & Tears				
Hi-De-Ho	8/17/70	8/31/70	11	6
Lucretia Mac Evil	10/4/70	11/2/70	13	7
Bloodstone				
Natural High	6/11/73	7/2/73	11	7
Bloom, Bobby				
Montego Bay	10/19/70	11/30/70	2	13
Blue Oyster Cult				
(Don't Fear) The Reaper	10/2/76	11/13/76	5	16
Blue Ridge Rangers				
Jambalaya (On The Bayou)	1/22/73	2/26/73	14	7
also see Creedence Clearwater Revival				
Blue Swede				
Hooked On A Feeling	3/2/74	3/30/74	1	15
Never My Love	9/21/74	10/19/74	8	6

Artist	Title	Debut	Peak	Pos	Wks
Blues Brothers					
	Soul Man	2/3/79	3/3/79	11	14
Blues Image					
	Ride Captain Ride	5/11/70	6/22/70	3	12
Booker T. & the MG's					
	Melting Pot	4/26/71	5/10/71	27	3
Boone, Daniel					
	Beautiful Sunday	8/7/72	9/25/72	10	11
Boone, Debby					
	You Light Up My Life	9/17/77	10/8/77	1	35
Bootsy's Rubber Band					
	Bootzilla	3/11/78	4/22/78	24	12
Boston					
	More Than A Feeling	10/16/76	12/4/76	2	18
	Long Time	2/12/77	3/26/77	8	14
	Peace Of Mind	5/21/77	7/9/77	10	13
	Don't Look Back	9/16/78	10/28/78	14	14
Bowie, David					
	Space Oddity	4/2/73	4/2/73	22	2
	Fame	9/20/75	10/18/75	3	15
	Golden Years	1/17/76	2/28/76	35	12
Boys In The Band					
	(How Bout A Little Hand For) The Boys In The Band	7/6/70	7/27/70	26	4
Brass Construction					
	Movin'	5/29/76	6/19/76	26	6
Bread					
	Make It With You	6/29/70	7/27/70	1	13
	It Don't Matter To Me	10/4/70	10/26/70	3	8
	Let Your Love Go	12/21/70	1/25/71	11	8
	If	3/22/71	4/26/71	2	10
	Mother Freedom	8/9/71	8/16/71	21	3
	Baby I'm-A Want You	10/25/71	11/29/71	2	11

Artist	Title	Debut	Peak	Pos	Wks
	Everything I Own	2/7/72	2/21/72	7	8
	Diary	5/15/72	6/5/72	15	6
	The Guitar Man	8/7/72	8/28/72	10	9
	Sweet Surrender	11/27/72	12/25/72	14	5
	Aubrey	2/26/73	3/19/73	16	6
	Lost Without Your Love	1/8/77	2/26/77	18	13

also see Gates, David

Bremers, Beverly
	Don't Say You Don't Remember	2/14/72	2/21/72	11	6

Brewer & Shipley
	One Toke Over The Line	2/8/71	3/29/71	4	11
	Tarkio Road	5/17/71	6/7/71	12	5

Brick
	Dazz	12/18/76	1/22/77	3	14
	Ain't Gonna' Hurt Nobody	3/4/78	3/25/78	29	9

Bridges, Alicia
	I Love The Nightlife (Disco 'Round)	12/9/78	1/27/79	8	26

Brighter Side Of Darkness
	Love Jones	1/22/73	1/29/73	14	3

Bristol, Johnny
	Hang On In There Baby	8/10/74	8/31/74	12	5

Brotherhood Of Man
	United We Stand	5/11/70	6/29/70	15	10

also see Edison Lighthouse, First Class, the Pipkins and White Plains

Brothers Johnson
	I'll Be Good To You	7/3/76	7/31/76	14	10
	Strawberry Letter 23	8/13/77	10/15/77	24	13

Brown, Chuck & the Soul Searchers
	Bustin' Loose Part 1	3/10/79	3/24/79	27	10

Brown, James
	Get On The Good Foot-Part 1	10/2/72	10/16/72	17	4

Brown, Peter
	Do Ya Wanna Get Funky With Me	8/27/77	10/22/77	3	18

Artist	Title	Debut	Peak	Pos	Wks
Brown, Peter with Betty Wright					
	Dance With Me	3/11/78	7/1/78	11	28
	Also see Wright, Betty				
Brown, Polly					
	Up In A Puff Of Smoke	2/22/75	3/22/75	9	5
Browne, Jackson					
	Doctor My Eyes	4/3/72	4/24/72	4	9
	Here Come Those Tears Again	2/26/77	3/26/77	31	7
	Running On Empty	4/8/78	5/13/78	14	14
Brownsville Station					
	Smokin' In The Boy's Room	11/24/73	1/12/74	2	13
	I'm The Leader Of The Gang	6/22/74	7/13/74	11	5
Bryson, Peabo					
	Reachin' For The Sky	4/1/78	4/22/78	41	3
	I'm So Into You	2/24/79	3/17/79	35	5
B.T. Express					
	Do It ('Til You're Satisfied)	11/30/74	12/21/74	8	6
	Express	3/29/75	4/12/75	16	3
	Shout It Out	3/18/78	3/18/78	44	1
Buffett, Jimmy					
	Margaritaville	6/4/77	8/13/77	8	17
Bullet					
	White Lies, Blue Eyes	12/27/71	1/17/72	5	9
Burdon, Eric & War					
	Spill The Wine	7/13/70	8/17/70	1	12
	also see War				
Butler, Jerry & Brenda Lee Eager					
	Ain't Understanding Mellow	1/31/72	2/28/72	17	6
	also see the Impressions				
Caldwell, Bobby					
	What You Won't Do For Love	1/27/79	3/3/79	26	15
Cale, J.J.					
	Crazy Mama	3/20/72	4/3/72	12	4

Artist Title	Debut	Peak	Pos	Wks
Campbell, Glen				
Honey Come Back	1/12/70	2/23/70	22	8
It's Only Make Believe	10/12/70	11/2/70	18	5
Dream Baby (How Long Must I Dream)	3/29/71	4/12/71	19	4
Rhinestone Cowboy	8/16/75	9/6/75	1	23
Country Boy (You Got Your Feet In L.A.)	12/20/75	1/3/76	12	10
Southern Nights	3/26/77	4/30/77	1	18
Sunflower	8/13/77	9/3/77	38	5
also see Gentry, Bobbie & Glen Campbell				
Canned Heat				
Let's Work Together	10/12/70	11/16/70	4	11
Captain & Tennille				
Love Will Keep Us Together	6/14/75	7/5/75	1	25
The Way I Want To Touch You	11/8/75	12/6/75	2	15
Lonely Night (Angel Face)	2/7/76	3/13/76	1	20
Shop Around	5/8/76	6/26/76	1	18
Muskrat Love	10/2/76	11/13/76	1	22
Can't Stop Dancin'	4/2/77	5/7/77	7	14
Come In From The Rain	6/18/77	7/16/77	24	8
You Never Done It Like That	10/28/78	12/2/78	21	10
Do That To Me One More Time	12/8/79	2/16/80	5	21
Captain Sky				
Wonder Worm	1/13/79	1/13/79	44	1
Carlton, Carl				
Everlasting Love	11/2/74	12/7/74	8	12
Carmen, Eric				
All By Myself	12/27/75	3/20/76	4	22
Never Gonna Fall In Love Again	5/22/76	7/3/76	7	14
Sunrise	9/11/76	10/9/76	35	8
She Did It	9/24/77	11/19/77	6	17
also see the Raspberries				
Carpenters				
Ticket To Ride	2/23/70	3/2/70	35	2
(They Long To Be) Close To You	6/29/70	7/20/70	1	13
We've Only Just Begun	9/28/70	10/26/70	2	11

Artist	Title	Debut	Peak	Pos	Wks
	For All We Know	2/8/71	3/15/71	4	9
	Rainy Days And Mondays	5/3/71	6/14/71	2	11
	Superstar	9/13/71	10/4/71	3	10
	Hurting Each Other	1/24/72	2/14/72	1	11
	It's Going To Take Some Time	5/8/72	6/12/72	9	8
	Goodbye To Love	7/31/72	8/28/72	7	8
	Sing	3/19/73	4/23/73	4	11
	Yesterday Once More	6/18/73	7/23/73	4	12
	Top Of The World	10/13/73	12/22/73	2	19
	I Won't Last A Day Without You	5/25/74	6/8/74	15	3
	Please Mr. Postman	12/14/74	1/18/75	1	17
	Only Yesterday	4/12/75	6/7/75	3	20
	There's A Kind Of A Hush (All Over The World)	4/10/76	5/8/76	25	8
	I Need To Be In Love	7/24/76	8/14/76	35	5

Carradine, Keith
| | I'm Easy | 7/3/76 | 8/14/76 | 4 | 14 |

Cars
| | Let's Go | 8/4/79 | 9/15/79 | 5 | 20 |

Carter, Clarence
| | Patches | 8/3/70 | 9/7/70 | 5 | 11 |

Cash, Johnny
| | What Is Truth | 4/13/70 | 5/11/70 | 16 | 7 |

Cash, Tommy
| | Six White Horses | 12/22/69 | 12/29/69 | 37 | 3 |

Cashman & West
| | American City Suite | 11/6/72 | 11/6/72 | 21 | 1 |

Cassidy, David
| | Cherish | 10/25/71 | 12/20/71 | 3 | 15 |
| | How Can I Be Sure | 6/5/72 | 6/19/72 | 16 | 3 |

also see the Partridge Family

Cassidy, Shaun
	Da Doo Ron Ron	5/28/77	6/18/77	1	23
	That's Rock 'N' Roll	8/13/77	10/1/77	1	26
	Hey Deanie	12/10/77	1/21/78	6	19
	Do You Believe In Magic	4/15/78	5/6/78	22	11

Artist Title	Debut	Peak	Pos	Wks
Castor, Jimmy, Bunch				
Troglodyte (Cave Man)	5/22/72	6/19/72	5	5
Chairmen of the Board				
Give Me Just A Little More Time	2/2/70	3/9/70	4	9
Pay To The Piper	12/14/70	1/4/71	13	6
Chakachas				
Jungle Fever	3/13/72	3/27/72	6	7
Chandler, Gene				
Groovy Situation	8/10/70	9/7/70	6	10
Get Down	12/23/78	1/27/79	19	15
Chapin, Harry				
Cat's In The Cradle	11/16/74	12/21/74	1	16
Chase				
Get It On	5/24/71	7/19/71	5	11
Cheap Trick				
Surrender	8/26/78	9/16/78	24	13
I Want You To Want Me	5/26/79	7/7/79	2	24
Dream Police	10/13/79	12/8/79	8	19
Cheech & Chong				
Basketball Jones Featuring Tyrone Shoelaces	9/22/73	11/3/73	2	12
Sister Mary Elephant (Shudd-Up!)	12/1/73	1/19/74	3	13
Earache My Eye Featuring Alice Bowie	9/7/74	9/28/74	1	11
Cher				
Gypsys, Tramps & Thieves	10/4/71	11/1/71	2	10
The Way Of Love	2/14/72	3/13/72	3	11
Living In A House Divided	6/5/72	7/3/72	16	6
Half-Breed	9/1/73	10/6/73	1	15
Dark Lady	1/19/74	3/2/74	3	13
Train Of Thought	6/22/74	7/6/74	10	4
Take Me Home	4/14/79	6/2/79	8	16
also see Sonny & Cher				

Artist	Title	Debut	Peak	Pos	Wks
Chic					
	Dance, Dance, Dance (Yowsah, Yowsah, Yowsah)	1/21/78	3/18/78	7	24
	Le Freak	12/2/78	12/30/78	1	26
	I Want Your Love	3/17/79	4/21/79	13	17
	Good Times	7/7/79	9/1/79	2	20
Chicago					
	Make Me Smile	5/11/70	6/22/70	7	10
	25 Or 6 To 4	8/3/70	8/31/70	2	9
	Does Anybody Really Know What Time It Is	11/23/70	12/14/70	3	8
	Free	3/8/71	3/22/71	13	5
	Beginnings	6/21/71	8/2/71	3	11
	/Colour My World	8/9/71	8/9/71	7	4
	Saturday In The Park	8/21/72	9/25/72	3	9
	Dialogue (Part I & II)	11/27/72	12/11/72	17	4
	Feelin' Stronger Every Day	6/11/73	8/25/73	4	16
	Just You 'N' Me	10/6/73	11/24/73	2	14
	(I've Been) Searchin' So Long	5/4/74	5/25/74	12	5
	Call On Me	8/17/74	8/24/74	23	3
	Wishing You Were Here	11/23/74	12/7/74	11	4
	Old Days	5/17/75	6/28/75	10	11
	If You Leave Me Now	8/21/76	9/18/76	1	20
	Baby, What A Big Surprise	10/22/77	11/26/77	12	12
	Alive Again	11/25/78	12/23/78	17	11
Chi-Lites					
	(For God's Sake) Give More Power To The People	5/3/71	5/24/71	17	5
	Have You Seen Her	11/1/71	12/13/71	1	13
	Oh Girl	4/17/72	5/22/72	1	13
Chocolate Milk					
	Girl Calling	6/3/78	7/15/78	23	12
Clapton, Eric					
	After Midnight	11/9/70	12/14/70	4	10
	I Shot The Sheriff	8/24/74	9/14/74	2	12
	Hello Old Friend	11/27/76	12/18/76	31	7
	Lay Down Sally	2/11/78	4/29/78	8	19
	Promises	1/27/79	2/17/79	30	8

Artist Title	Debut	Peak	Pos	Wks
Clay, Tom				
What The World Needs Now Is Love/Abraham, Martin And John	7/19/71	8/9/71	4	5
Cliff, Jimmy				
Wonderful World, Beautiful People	11/24/69	1/5/70	10	10
Clifford, Linda				
Runaway Love	6/3/78	7/22/78	19	15
Climax				
Precious And Few	1/24/72	2/14/72	2	9
Climax Blues Band				
Couldn't Get It Right	4/2/77	6/11/77	4	17
Cochise				
Love's Made A Fool Of You	4/19/71	5/31/71	10	8
Cocker, Joe				
The Letter	4/27/70	6/1/70	2	10
Cry Me A River	11/2/70	11/23/70	7	6
High Time We Went	5/31/71	7/12/71	8	9
You Are So Beautiful	3/15/75	4/12/75	7	13
Coffey, Dennis & the Detroit Guitar Band				
Scorpio	11/29/71	1/17/72	4	13
Taurus	3/27/72	4/24/72	16	6
Cole, Natalie				
This Will Be	12/27/75	12/27/75	40	2
Sophisticated Lady (She's A Different Lady)	7/3/76	8/14/76	33	9
I've Got Love On My Mind	3/12/77	4/23/77	14	13
Our Love	2/4/78	4/8/78	11	18
Annie Mae	7/29/78	8/12/78	32	7
Collins, Dave & Ansil				
Double Barrel	5/24/71	6/28/71	4	8
Collins, Judy				
Send In The Clowns	11/5/77	12/17/77	13	12
Coltrane, Chi				
Thunder And Lightning	10/9/72	11/20/72	12	7

Artist	Title	Debut	Peak	Pos	Wks
Commodores					
	Sweet Love	3/20/76	5/8/76	17	12
	Just To Be Close To You	10/16/76	11/20/76	19	10
	Easy	7/30/77	8/27/77	27	9
	Brick House	10/1/77	11/12/77	21	11
	Three Times A Lady	7/15/78	9/2/78	1	23
	Sail On	9/15/79	11/3/79	5	20
	Still	11/3/79	12/15/79	5	19
Como, Perry					
	And I Love You So	6/4/73	6/4/73	28	3
Con Funk Shun					
	Ffun	2/11/78	3/18/78	27	9
Connors, Norman					
	You Are My Starship	9/25/76	11/13/76	23	12
Conti, Bill					
	Gonna Fly Now	4/23/77	5/28/77	1	18
Coolidge, Rita					
	(Your Love Has Lifted Me) Higher And Higher	6/25/77	8/20/77	2	20
	We're All Alone	10/8/77	12/3/77	5	17
	The Way You Do The Things You Do	3/18/78	4/1/78	38	6
	You	8/12/78	9/9/78	21	12
Cooper, Alice					
	Eighteen	3/15/71	4/12/71	2	8
	Elected	11/6/72	11/6/72	26	1
	No More Mr. Nice Guy	5/28/73	6/25/73	16	6
	Teenage Lament '74	12/22/73	2/16/74	13	11
	I Never Cry	10/30/76	12/4/76	29	9
	You And Me	7/9/77	9/17/77	10	16
	How You Gonna See Me Now	12/23/78	1/20/79	26	11
Cornelius Brothers & Sister Rose					
	Treat Her Like A Lady	4/12/71	5/31/71	4	10
	Too Late To Turn Back Now	6/5/72	7/17/72	2	12
	Don't Ever Be Lonely (A Poor Little Fool Like Me)	10/9/72	10/30/72	21	4

Artist Title	Debut	Peak	Pos	Wks
Coven				
One Tin Soldier, The Legend Of Billy Jack	12/1/73	1/5/74	1	16
Creedence Clearwater Revival				
Fortunate Son	10/27/69	12/8/69	3	12
/Down On The Corner	11/10/69	12/8/69	3	10
Who'll Stop The Rain	1/19/70	2/16/70	3	12
/Travelin' Band	1/19/70	2/16/70	3	6
Up Around The Bend	4/13/70	5/25/70	1	13
Lookin' Out My Back Door	8/3/70	9/14/70	1	13
Have You Ever Seen The Rain	1/18/71	2/22/71	4	10
Sweet Hitch-Hiker	7/12/71	8/16/71	3	9
Someday Never Comes	6/5/72	6/12/72	25	2
also see the Blue Ridge Rangers				
Croce, Jim				
You Don't Mess Around With Jim	7/24/72	9/4/72	6	11
Operator (That's Not The Way It Feels)	11/6/72	12/11/72	14	7
Bad, Bad Leroy Brown	6/4/73	7/16/73	1	12
I Got A Name	10/6/73	12/8/73	1	18
Time In A Bottle	12/1/73	1/12/74	3	12
I'll Have To Say I Love You In A Song	4/20/74	5/4/74	8	4
Crosby, Stills, Nash & Young				
Woodstock	3/16/70	5/11/70	4	12
Teach Your Children	6/1/70	7/6/70	14	7
Our House	10/19/70	10/26/70	27	2
Graham Nash & David Crosby				
Immigration Man	6/12/72	6/19/72	27	2
Crosby, Stills & Nash				
Just A Song Before I Go	7/2/77	8/27/77	11	14
also see Stills, Stephen and Young, Neil				
Cross Country				
In The Midnight Hour	9/22/73	10/6/73	32	5
Crow				
Evil Woman Don't Play Your Games With Me	11/10/69	12/22/69	6	11
Don't Try To Lay No Boogie Woogie On The "King Of Rock & Roll"	11/9/70	11/16/70	16	3

Artist	Title	Debut	Peak	Pos	Wks
Cummings, Burton					
	Stand Tall	11/6/76	1/8/77	3	19
	also see the Guess Who				
Cymarron					
	Rings	6/28/71	7/26/71	17	6
Daddy Dewdrop					
	Chick-A-Boom (Don't Ya Jes' Love It)	4/5/71	5/3/71	5	8
Dahl, Steve & Teenage Radiation					
	Do You Think I'm Disco	9/8/79	10/6/79	5	19
Damon's, Liz, Orient Express					
	1900 Yesterday	1/4/71	1/25/71	10	7
Dana, Vic					
	If I Never Knew Your Name	12/15/69	2/9/70	7	13
	Red Red Wine	5/4/70	5/11/70	36	3
Daniels, Charlie					
	Uneasy Rider	7/2/73	8/18/73	8	8
	The Devil Went Down To Georgia	8/11/79	9/22/79	2	23
Davis, Mac					
	Baby Don't Get Hooked On Me	8/14/72	9/25/72	1	12
	Stop And Smell The Roses	9/28/74	10/26/74	8	6
Davis, Paul					
	I Go Crazy	11/12/77	12/3/77	31	5
Davis, Jr., Sammy					
	The Candy Man	5/8/72	6/26/72	2	11
Davis, Tyrone					
	Turn Back The Hands Of Time	3/23/70	4/27/70	10	11
	Get On Up	5/20/78	6/3/78	32	6
	In The Mood	4/14/79	5/12/79	38	8
Dawn					
	Candida	8/24/70	9/28/70	1	12
	Knock Three Times	11/23/70	12/28/70	1	13
	I Play And Sing	3/29/71	4/19/71	3	7
	Summer Sand	6/21/71	7/26/71	10	7

Artist Title	Debut	Peak	Pos	Wks
Dawn featuring Tony Orlando				
What Are You Doing Sunday	9/27/71	10/25/71	10	8
Tie A Yellow Ribbon Round The Ole Oak Tree	3/26/73	4/30/73	1	10
Say, Has Anybody Seen My Sweet Gypsy Rose	7/23/73	9/22/73	8	11
Tony Orlando & Dawn				
Who's In The Strawberry Patch With Sally	12/8/73	12/22/73	30	5
He Don't Love You (Like I Love You)	3/29/75	5/10/75	4	16
Mornin' Beautiful	8/2/75	8/16/75	19	3
Daybreak				
Good Morning Freedom	6/1/70	7/6/70	19	7
Deal, Bill & the Rhondels				
Nothing Succeeds Like Success	4/6/70	4/20/70	25	4
Dean, Jimmy				
I.O.U.	5/22/76	6/5/76	21	5
Deep Purple				
Smoke On The Water	6/18/73	7/30/73	5	12
Dees, Rick & his Cast of Idiots				
Disco Duck (Part 1)	9/11/76	10/9/76	1	24
DeFranco Family featuring Tony DeFranco				
Heartbeat—It's A Lovebeat	9/22/73	10/20/73	1	17
Abra-Ca-Dabra	12/29/73	2/16/74	5	14
Delaney & Bonnie				
Never Ending Song Of Love	7/5/71	8/2/71	2	8
Only You Know And I Know	10/11/71	11/1/71	7	8
Delegation				
Oh Honey	3/31/79	4/21/79	27	10
Delfonics				
Didn't I (Blow Your Mind This Time)	2/2/70	3/2/70	7	10
Dells				
Give Your Baby A Standing Ovation	6/18/73	7/2/73	26	3
Denver, John				
Take Me Home, Country Roads	6/28/71	8/16/71	2	12
Rocky Mountain High	1/15/73	3/12/73	6	10

Artist	Title	Debut	Peak	Pos	Wks
	Sunshine On My Shoulders	2/16/74	3/9/74	4	11
	Annie's Song	7/6/74	7/20/74	2	11
	Back Home Again	11/9/74	11/23/74	9	4
	Sweet Surrender	2/1/75	2/15/75	13	4
	Thank God I'm A Country Boy	5/17/75	6/28/75	6	14
	I'm Sorry	9/27/75	11/1/75	4	14
	Fly Away	12/27/75	2/7/76	19	10

Deodato
	Also Sprach Zarathustra (2001)	2/19/73	4/2/73	1	9

Derringer, Rick
	Rock And Roll, Hoochie Koo	3/16/74	3/16/74	20	2

Detroit Emeralds
	Baby Let Me Take You (In My Arms)	7/31/72	8/28/72	18	6

DeVaughn, William
	Be Thankful For What You Got	6/22/74	6/22/74	22	3

DeVorzon, Barry & Perry Botkin, Jr.
	Nadia's Theme (The Young And The Restless)	10/30/76	12/25/76	1	22

Diamond, Neil
	Holly Holy	10/13/69	11/17/69	2	14
	Until It's Time For You To Go	2/23/70	3/2/70	34	3
	Shilo	3/16/70	4/13/70	14	6
	Soolaimon (African Trilogy II)	4/27/70	5/18/70	22	7
	Solitary Man	8/24/70	9/7/70	18	7
	Cracklin' Rosie	8/31/70	10/4/70	1	11
	He Ain't Heavy... He's My Brother	11/23/70	12/21/70	12	6
	I Am... I Said	3/8/71	4/19/71	2	10
	/Done Too Soon	5/10/71	5/10/71	32	1
	Stones	11/8/71	12/13/71	9	9
	/Crunchy Granola Suite	11/22/71	12/13/71	9	8
	Song Sung Blue	5/8/72	6/26/72	1	12
	Play Me	9/4/72	10/2/72	10	7
	Walk On Water	12/4/72	1/8/73	20	5
	"Cherry Cherry" from Hot August Night	4/23/73	5/7/73	20	5
	Be	10/20/73	12/1/73	8	10

Artist	Title	Debut	Peak	Pos	Wks
	Longfellow Serenade	11/9/74	12/7/74	5	13
	If You Know What I Mean	8/14/76	9/4/76	28	7
	Desiree	12/31/77	2/11/78	22	13
	also see Streisand, Barbra & Neil Diamond				

Dibango, Manu
	Soul Makossa	6/25/73	7/9/73	28	3

Dire Straits
	Sultans Of Swing	3/17/79	4/14/79	9	14

Donaldson, Bo & the Heywoods
	Billy, Don't Be A Hero	5/18/74	6/8/74	1	14
	Who Do You Think You Are	8/31/74	9/28/74	5	13

Doobie Brothers
	Listen To The Music	10/2/72	11/6/72	6	9
	Long Train Runnin'	5/28/73	7/9/73	2	11
	China Grove	9/8/73	10/13/73	5	12
	Another Park, Another Sunday	6/15/74	6/15/74	17	1
	Black Water	2/1/75	2/22/75	1	18
	Take Me In Your Arms (Rock Me)	5/31/75	7/12/75	8	14
	Takin' It To The Streets	5/22/76	6/26/76	15	11
	What A Fool Believes	3/3/79	4/14/79	2	25
	Minute By Minute	6/16/79	7/14/79	19	11

Doors
	Love Her Madly	4/5/71	5/10/71	4	10
	Riders On The Storm	7/5/71	8/16/71	1	11

Douglas, Carl
	Kung Fu Fighting	11/16/74	12/7/74	1	17

Douglas, Carol
	Doctor's Orders	1/18/75	2/22/75	7	11

Dr. Buzzard's Original "Savannah" Band
	Whispering/Cherchez La Femme/Se Si Bon	11/20/76	12/25/76	22	9

Dr. Hook & the Medicine Show
	Sylvia's Mother	4/24/72	6/5/72	2	12

Dr. Hook
	Only Sixteen	2/21/76	4/3/76	7	15

Artist	Title	Debut	Peak	Pos	Wks
	A Little Bit More	8/28/76	10/23/76	27	11
	Sharing The Night Together	12/2/78	1/20/79	14	16
	When You're In Love With A Beautiful Woman	7/28/79	9/1/79	7	16

Dr. John
	Right Place Wrong Time	5/14/73	7/2/73	5	10

Dramatics
	Whatcha See Is Whatcha Get	8/16/71	8/30/71	10	6
	In The Rain	3/27/72	4/24/72	7	8

Duke, George
	Dukey Stick	5/20/78	6/10/78	24	11

Dundas, David
	Jeans On	11/13/76	12/4/76	34	5

Dylan, Bob
	Watching The River Flow	6/28/71	7/19/71	16	5
	Knockin' On Heaven's Door	10/13/73	11/24/73	19	10
	Hurricane (Part I)	1/24/76	2/7/76	38	3

Dyson, Ronnie
	(If You Let Me Make Love To You Then) Why Can't I Touch You	7/6/70	8/10/70	3	10
	One Man Band (Plays All Alone)	4/9/73	4/16/73	18	3

Eagles
	Take It Easy	6/19/72	7/17/72	9	7
	Witchy Woman	10/23/72	11/13/72	9	7
	Peaceful Easy Feeling	2/12/73	3/5/73	19	4
	Best Of My Love	1/11/75	2/8/75	3	15
	One Of These Nights	7/12/75	8/9/75	7	13
	Lyin' Eyes	10/11/75	11/15/75	4	14
	Take It To The Limit	1/17/76	2/28/76	24	13
	New Kid In Town	12/25/76	2/19/77	2	18
	Hotel California	3/19/77	5/7/77	3	18
	Life In The Fast Lane	5/21/77	7/9/77	8	13
	Heartache Tonight	9/29/79	11/17/79	4	22
	The Long Run	12/15/79	2/2/80	14	14

also see Poco and Walsh, Joe

Artist Title	Debut	Peak	Pos	Wks
Earth, Wind & Fire				
Shining Star	5/24/75	6/7/75	9	7
Sing A Song	1/3/76	1/24/76	14	12
Getaway	9/11/76	10/9/76	23	8
Got To Get You Into My Life	8/12/78	9/16/78	17	15
September	12/16/78	2/10/79	3	22
After The Love Has Gone	8/11/79	9/15/79	12	18
Earth, Wind & Fire with the Emotions				
Boogie Wonderland	6/16/79	7/14/79	12	18
also see the Emotions				
Edison Lighthouse				
Love Grows (Where My Rosemary Goes)	2/9/70	3/16/70	1	13
also see the Brotherhood of Man, First Class, the Pipkins and White Plains				
Edmunds, Dave				
I Hear You Knocking	12/14/70	1/18/71	1	12
Edward Bear				
Last Song	2/5/73	3/12/73	3	10
Edwards, Jonathan				
Sunshine	11/29/71	12/27/71	2	13
Egan, Walter				
Magnet And Steel	8/19/78	10/21/78	6	19
8th Day				
She's Not Just Another Woman	4/26/71	6/7/71	8	8
El Chicano				
Viva Tirado—Part I	4/20/70	5/18/70	19	9
Brown Eyed Girl	6/19/72	6/26/72	25	2
Tell Her She's Lovely	12/8/73	1/5/74	21	8
Elbert, Donnie				
Where Did Our Love Go	12/6/71	12/27/71	7	8
I Can't Help Myself (Sugar Pie, Honey Bunch)	2/7/72	3/6/72	12	8
Electric Light Orchestra				
Roll Over Beethoven	8/11/73	9/1/73	8	8
Can't Get It Out Of My Head	3/1/75	3/29/75	14	5
Evil Woman	12/27/75	2/14/76	6	17

Artist	Title	Debut	Peak	Pos	Wks
	Strange Magic	4/24/76	5/29/76	33	8
	Livin' Thing	11/13/76	12/25/76	11	14
	Do Ya	3/5/77	4/16/77	24	10
	Telephone Line	7/23/77	9/17/77	15	14
	Turn To Stone	12/17/77	2/4/78	11	18
	Sweet Talkin' Woman	4/15/78	5/27/78	21	14
	Shine A Little Love	6/30/79	7/28/79	13	14
	Don't Bring Me Down	8/4/79	10/13/79	5	24

Elliman, Yvonne

	Love Me	11/20/76	12/25/76	18	9
	Hello Stranger	5/7/77	6/4/77	28	8
	If I Can't Have You	3/25/78	5/6/78	9	16

Emotions

	Best Of My Love	7/16/77	9/17/77	1	19

also see Earth, Wind & Fire & the Emotions

Enchantment

	Gloria	4/2/77	4/30/77	34	6
	It's You That I Need	3/4/78	4/8/78	25	12

England Dan & John Ford Coley

	I'd Really Love To See You Tonight	7/10/76	9/11/76	3	19
	Nights Are Forever Without You	10/30/76	12/18/76	7	14
	It's Sad To Belong	6/25/77	7/30/77	15	11
	Gone Too Far	12/3/77	12/17/77	39	3
	We'll Never Have To Say Goodbye Again	4/15/78	5/13/78	28	9

Ernie (Jim Henson)

	Rubber Duckie	8/31/70	9/21/70	6	5

Essex, David

	Rock On	2/9/74	3/16/74	1	11

Exile

	Kiss You All Over	9/2/78	10/21/78	1	25

Faces

	Stay With Me	1/3/72	2/7/72	4	10

also see Stewart, Rod

Artist　Title	Debut	Peak	Pos	Wks
Fairchild, Barbara				
Teddy Bear Song	5/21/73	5/21/73	24	2
Faith, Hope & Charity				
So Much Love	7/6/70	7/6/70	38	1
Fancy				
Wild Thing	7/20/74	8/24/74	6	10
Fanny				
Charity Ball	10/4/71	10/25/71	3	9
Fargo, Donna				
The Happiest Girl In The Whole U.S.A.	6/12/72	8/14/72	11	13
Funny Face	11/27/72	1/8/73	5	9
Fatback Band				
I Like Girls	8/26/78	10/14/78	21	13
Fender, Freddy				
Before The Next Teardrop Falls	6/7/75	6/7/75	13	1
Secret Love	12/27/75	12/27/75	36	2
Ferguson, Jay				
Thunder Island	1/21/78	4/15/78	14	19
also see Jo Jo Gunne				
Ferrante & Teicher				
Midnight Cowboy	11/17/69	1/12/70	6	12
Fifth Dimension				
Blowing Away	1/5/70	2/2/70	9	7
Puppet Man	4/20/70	5/18/70	14	7
Save The Country	6/22/70	7/6/70	17	5
One Less Bell To Answer	11/16/70	12/14/70	2	11
Love's Lines, Angles And Rhymes	2/22/71	3/15/71	9	6
Light Sings	5/24/71	6/14/71	16	5
Never My Love	10/4/71	11/1/71	10	8
(Last Night) I Didn't Get To Sleep At All	5/8/72	6/12/72	6	11
If I Could Reach You	10/9/72	11/27/72	7	10
also see McCoo, Marilyn & Billy Davis, Jr.				

Artist	Title	Debut	Peak	Pos	Wks
Firefall					
	You Are The Woman	10/16/76	12/11/76	2	16
	Cinderella	4/30/77	5/14/77	32	7
	Just Remember I Love You	9/17/77	11/5/77	4	15
	Strange Way	12/16/78	1/13/79	26	10
	also see Jo Jo Gunne				
First Choice					
	Armed And Extremely Dangerous	4/30/73	4/30/73	25	2
First Class					
	Beach Baby	9/7/74	10/26/74	1	15
	also see the Brotherhood of Man, Edison Lighthouse, the Pipkins and White Plains				
Five Flights Up					
	Do What You Wanna Do	9/14/70	10/4/70	6	7
Five Man Electrical Band					
	Signs	7/12/71	8/23/71	2	12
	Absolutely Right	10/4/71	11/15/71	5	10
Five Stairsteps					
	O-o-h Child	6/15/70	7/20/70	4	12
5000 Volts					
	I'm On Fire	12/27/75	12/27/75	37	2
Flack, Roberta					
	The First Time Ever I Saw Your Face	3/20/72	4/10/72	1	12
	Killing Me Softly With His Song	2/12/73	3/5/73	1	11
	Jesse	10/13/73	11/3/73	31	4
	Feel Like Makin' Love	8/3/74	8/24/74	4	11
Flack, Roberta & Donny Hathaway					
	Where Is The Love	6/26/72	8/14/72	4	10
	The Closer I Get To You	3/18/78	5/20/78	6	21
Flaming Ember					
	Westbound #9	7/13/70	7/27/70	21	4
	I'm Not My Brother's Keeper	12/14/70	12/14/70	30	1
Flash Cadillac & the Continental Kids					
	Did You Boogie (With Your Baby)	10/9/76	10/30/76	33	6

Artist	Title	Debut	Peak	Pos	Wks
Fleetwood Mac					
	Over My Head	12/27/75	2/28/76	11	18
	Rhiannon (Will You Ever Win)	4/3/76	5/8/76	6	15
	Say You Love Me	7/17/76	8/21/76	9	15
	Go Your Own Way	1/22/77	3/12/77	9	15
	Dreams	4/30/77	6/4/77	7	18
	Don't Stop	7/30/77	9/17/77	8	17
	You Make Loving Fun	10/29/77	12/17/77	10	14
	Tusk	9/29/79	11/10/79	6	20
also see Welch, Bob					
Floaters					
	Float On	8/6/77	9/24/77	23	11
Floyd, King					
	Groove Me	1/18/71	2/8/71	15	6
Focus					
	Hocus Pocus	5/7/73	6/4/73	5	8
Fogelberg, Dan					
	Part Of The Plan	3/1/75	3/22/75	18	4
Foghat					
	Slow Ride	3/6/76	4/10/76	8	15
	I Just Want To Make Love To You	10/15/77	11/19/77	15	12
Foreigner					
	Feels Like The First Time	4/16/77	6/25/77	3	20
	Cold As Ice	8/20/77	10/22/77	6	17
	Long, Long Way From Home	1/7/78	2/25/78	16	14
	Hot Blooded	7/29/78	9/30/78	3	30
	Double Vision	11/4/78	12/2/78	9	20
	Dirty White Boy	10/20/79	11/17/79	25	9
	Head Games	12/1/79	1/12/80	16	12
Fortunes					
	Here Comes That Rainy Day Feeling Again	6/14/71	7/5/71	3	6
Four Seasons					
	Who Loves You	11/1/75	11/29/75	2	15
	December, 1963 (Oh, What A Night)	1/10/76	2/28/76	1	24
also see Valli, Frankie					

Artist	Title	Debut	Peak	Pos	Wks
Four Tops					
	It's All In The Game	5/18/70	7/6/70	16	9
	Still Water (Love)	11/2/70	11/16/70	19	4
	Keeper Of The Castle	12/4/72	1/15/73	7	9
	Ain't No Woman (Like The One I've Got)	3/5/73	4/9/73	2	10
	Are You Man Enough	8/18/73	9/1/73	15	7
	also see the Supremes & the Four Tops				
Foxy					
	Get Off	8/26/78	11/25/78	6	28
Frampton, Peter					
	Show Me The Way	4/3/76	5/8/76	8	14
	Baby, I Love Your Way	8/7/76	9/18/76	6	14
	Do You Feel Like We Do	10/9/76	11/20/76	9	14
	I'm In You	6/4/77	7/23/77	2	16
	Signed, Sealed, Delivered (I'm Yours)	9/10/77	10/22/77	9	13
Franklin, Aretha					
	Call Me	3/2/70	4/6/70	28	7
	You're All I Need To Get By	3/15/71	3/29/71	20	3
	Bridge Over Troubled Water	4/26/71	5/24/71	11	6
	Spanish Harlem	8/9/71	9/6/71	1	11
	Rock Steady	11/1/71	11/15/71	16	4
	Day Dreaming	3/20/72	5/8/72	2	12
	Angel	9/1/73	9/8/73	28	4
	Until You Come Back To Me (That's What I'm Gonna Do)	2/16/74	3/2/74	15	3
	Something He Can Feel	6/26/76	7/24/76	26	10
Free					
	All Right Now	9/14/70	10/4/70	2	10
	Stealer	11/16/70	12/21/70	19	5
	also see Bad Company				
Free Movement					
	I've Found Someone Of My Own	9/27/71	10/25/71	2	9
Friedman, Dean					
	Ariel	6/11/77	8/20/77	4	19

Artist　Title	Debut	Peak	Pos	Wks
Friends of Distinction				
Love Or Let Me Be Lonely	4/6/70	5/18/70	9	12
Frijid Pink				
House Of The Rising Sun	2/9/70	3/9/70	8	11
Funkadelic				
One Nation Under A Groove—Part I	9/16/78	11/11/78	12	18
Fuzz				
I Love You For All Seasons	4/12/71	5/10/71	12	6
Gallery				
Nice To Be With You	5/1/72	6/19/72	1	12
I Believe In Music	10/16/72	11/13/72	14	7
Big City Miss Ruth Ann	2/19/73	3/19/73	15	5
Garfunkel, Art				
All I Know	9/29/73	11/10/73	6	12
I Only Have Eyes For You	12/27/75	12/27/75	43	1
Garfunkel, Art with James Taylor & Paul Simon				
(What A) Wonderful World	3/25/78	4/22/78	36	5
also see Simon, Paul; Simon & Garfunkel and Taylor, James				
Garrett, Leif				
Surfin' USA	10/22/77	11/5/77	30	6
Runaround Sue	11/19/77	1/7/78	1	17
Gary's Gang				
Keep On Dancin'	4/28/79	6/2/79	23	10
Gates, David				
Goodbye Girl	4/15/78	5/13/78	13	15
also see Bread				
Gaye, Marvin				
How Can I Forget	1/12/70	1/26/70	28	3
What's Going On	2/22/71	3/22/71	3	9
Mercy Mercy Me (The Ecology)	7/5/71	8/9/71	3	9
Inner City Blues (Make Me Wanna Holler)	10/18/71	11/15/71	6	7
Trouble Man	1/8/73	2/5/73	9	7
Let's Get It On	7/30/73	9/8/73	1	15

Artist	Title	Debut	Peak	Pos	Wks
	I Want You	6/26/76	7/17/76	30	6
	Got To Give It Up (Pt. I)	5/7/77	6/4/77	20	11
Gayle, Crystal					
	Don't It Make My Brown Eyes Blue	10/8/77	12/10/77	1	21
	Half The Way	12/8/79	12/29/79	22	10
Gaynor, Gloria					
	Never Can Say Goodbye	1/11/75	2/8/75	8	11
	I Will Survive	1/20/79	3/31/79	1	27
	Anybody Wanna Party	8/11/79	9/1/79	34	9
Geddes, David					
	Run Joey Run	8/23/75	9/20/75	2	13
	The Last Game Of The Season (A Blind Man In The Bleachers)	12/27/75	12/27/75	32	2
Geils, J., Band					
	Looking For A Love	12/20/71	1/17/72	18	7
	Give It To Me	5/21/73	6/25/73	17	7
Genesis					
	Follow You Follow Me	7/29/78	8/19/78	32	8
Gentry, Bobbie & Glen Campbell					
	All I Have To Do Is Dream	2/2/70	3/16/70	11	9
also see Campbell, Glen					
Gentrys					
	Why Should I Cry	2/9/70	2/23/70	31	3
Gibb, Andy					
	I Just Want To Be Your Everything	6/11/77	8/13/77	1	25
	(Love Is) Thicker Than Water	1/21/78	3/4/78	2	23
	Shadow Dancing	5/6/78	6/10/78	1	24
	An Everlasting Love	8/12/78	9/16/78	11	14
	(Our Love) Don't Throw It All Away	11/25/78	1/27/79	11	17
Gilder, Nick					
	Hot Child In The City	9/30/78	11/25/78	1	24
Giorgio					
	Son Of My Father	2/28/72	3/27/72	23	6

Artist	Title	Debut	Peak	Pos	Wks
Glass Bottle					
	I Ain't Got Time Anymore	9/6/71	9/13/71	17	3
Glitter, Gary					
	Rock And Roll Part 2	8/14/72	9/18/72	5	8
Godspell					
	Day By Day	6/26/72	8/7/72	10	9
Gold, Andrew					
	Lonely Boy	4/30/77	6/25/77	2	18
	Thank You For Being A Friend	5/6/78	5/27/78	30	10
Golden Earring					
	Radar Love	7/13/74	8/10/74	4	10
Goldsboro, Bobby					
	Watching Scotty Grow	1/11/71	2/8/71	4	9
	Summer (The First Time)	10/13/73	11/10/73	32	6
Goodman, Dickie					
	Energy Crisis '74	3/9/74	3/9/74	12	3
	Mr. Jaws	9/13/75	10/11/75	1	8
GQ					
	Disco Nights (Rock-Freak)	3/24/79	5/26/79	14	21
	I Do Love You	9/29/79	10/27/79	26	10
Grand Funk Railroad					
	Closer To Home	9/7/70	9/7/70	31	1
	Rock 'N Roll Soul	11/20/72	11/20/72	26	1
Grand Funk					
	We're An American Band	7/30/73	9/22/73	1	13
	Walk Like A Man	12/22/73	2/2/74	22	9
	The Loco-motion	4/6/74	5/4/74	1	14
	Some Kind Of Wonderful	2/8/75	3/8/75	6	12
	Bad Time	5/3/75	6/21/75	4	15
Grass Roots					
	Heaven Knows	11/17/69	12/15/69	22	8
	Walking Through The Country	3/2/70	3/16/70	35	3
	Temptation Eyes	2/15/71	2/22/71	23	4
	Sooner Or Later	6/21/71	7/26/71	5	8

Artist	Title	Debut	Peak	Pos	Wks
	Two Divided By Love	10/25/71	11/22/71	9	7
	Glory Bound	2/28/72	3/20/72	9	8
	The Runway	7/24/72	7/24/72	24	1

Gray, Dobie
	Drift Away	4/9/73	5/21/73	5	10

Greaves, R.B.
	Always Something There To Remind Me	1/19/70	2/9/70	19	6

Green, Al
	Tired Of Being Alone	9/13/71	11/8/71	3	12
	Let's Stay Together	12/20/71	1/24/72	2	13
	Look What You Done For Me	4/10/72	5/22/72	3	10
	I'm Still In Love With You	7/24/72	9/11/72	2	10
	You Ought To Be With Me	11/6/72	12/11/72	3	11
	Call Me (Come Back Home)	3/12/73	4/2/73	10	6
	Here I Am (Come And Take Me)	8/18/73	9/1/73	18	4
	Sha-La-La (Make Me Happy)	12/7/74	12/21/74	12	4

Greenbaum, Norman
	Spirit In The Sky	2/23/70	3/23/70	1	12

Groce, Larry
	Junk Food Junkie	2/28/76	4/3/76	21	10

Gross, Henry
	Shannon	4/10/76	6/5/76	2	18

Guess Who
	No Time	1/5/70	1/26/70	2	10
	American Woman	3/16/70	5/4/70	1	14
	/No Sugar Tonight	4/13/70	5/4/70	1	10
	Hand Me Down World	7/20/70	8/31/70	7	9
	Share The Land	10/26/70	12/7/70	3	10
	Hang On To Your Life	2/1/71	2/15/71	15	5
	Albert Flasher	6/14/71	6/14/71	31	1
	Rain Dance	9/27/71	10/11/71	24	3
	Star Baby	5/11/74	5/25/74	3	12
	Clap For The Wolfman	10/5/74	10/26/74	12	7
	Dancin' Fool	1/4/75	2/1/75	14	5

also see Bachman-Turner Overdrive and Cummings, Burton

Artist Title	Debut	Peak	Pos	Wks
Gunhill Road				
Back When My Hair Was Short	6/4/73	7/2/73	17	5
Guthrie, Arlo				
The City Of New Orleans	9/25/72	10/2/72	22	5
Hall, Daryl & John Oates				
Sara Smile	5/8/76	7/10/76	9	21
She's Gone	9/4/76	10/23/76	9	14
Rich Girl	2/12/77	4/16/77	1	22
Back Together Again	5/28/77	6/18/77	32	5
Hall, Tom T.				
I Love	1/19/74	2/23/74	25	6
Hamilton, Joe Frank & Reynolds				
Don't Pull Your Love	5/24/71	7/12/71	3	12
Annabella	8/30/71	9/13/71	23	3
Fallin' In Love	8/23/75	9/13/75	1	14
Winners And Losers	12/13/75	12/27/75	11	11
Hamlisch, Marvin				
The Entertainer	4/27/74	5/4/74	3	8
Hammond, Albert				
It Never Rains In Southern California	9/25/72	12/25/72	3	17
Happenings				
Lullaby In The Rain	5/3/71	5/3/71	32	1
Harrison, George				
My Sweet Lord	11/23/70	12/7/70	1	11
What Is Life	3/1/71	3/29/71	5	8
Deep Blue	8/16/71	9/13/71	15	6
Give Me Love (Give Me Peace On Earth)	5/14/73	7/2/73	2	10
This Song	11/27/76	1/15/77	7	14
Crackerbox Palace	2/5/77	3/12/77	15	12
Blow Away	4/14/79	5/26/79	16	17
also see the Beatles				
Havens, Richie				
Here Comes The Sun	4/12/71	5/17/71	5	9

Artist	Title	Debut	Peak	Pos	Wks
Hayes, Isaac					
	Theme From Shaft	10/11/71	11/8/71	1	13
	Don't Let Go	12/1/79	12/29/79	18	15
Head, Murray with the Trinidad Singers					
	Superstar	4/26/71	5/10/71	7	6
Heart					
	Crazy On You	6/12/76	8/7/76	3	18
	Magic Man	8/28/76	10/9/76	7	14
	Dreamboat Annie	12/11/76	1/29/77	8	15
	Barracuda	6/18/77	7/30/77	6	16
	Straight On	12/9/78	12/23/78	28	9
Heatherton, Joey					
	Gone	7/24/72	8/7/72	23	4
Heatwave					
	Boogie Nights	9/24/77	11/26/77	1	23
	Always And Forever	1/28/78	3/11/78	19	23
	The Groove Line	4/29/78	6/17/78	6	23
Henderson, Michael					
	Take Me I'm Yours	9/30/78	10/28/78	35	6
High Inergy					
	You Can't Turn Me Off (In The Middle Of Turning Me On)	12/31/77	1/28/78	33	8
Hill, Dan					
	Sometimes When We Touch	1/7/78	3/11/78	6	20
Hodge, Chris					
	We're On Our Way	6/19/72	6/26/72	17	3
Hollies					
	He Ain't Heavy, He's My Brother	1/26/70	2/16/70	13	10
	Long Cool Woman (In A Black Dress)	7/10/72	9/4/72	2	12
	Long Dark Road	12/18/72	12/25/72	26	2
	The Air That I Breathe	7/13/74	8/24/74	2	13
Holman, Eddie					
	Hey There Lonely Girl	12/29/69	2/2/70	3	13
	Don't Stop Now	4/13/70	4/20/70	37	2

Artist	Title	Debut	Peak	Pos	Wks

Holmes, Clint
| | Playground In My Mind | 5/21/73 | 6/11/73 | 8 | 15 |

Holmes, Rupert
| | Escape (The Pina Colada Song) | 12/1/79 | 1/12/80 | 1 | 20 |

Honey Cone
	Want Ads	4/19/71	6/14/71	1	12
	Stick-Up	8/9/71	9/20/71	5	11
	One Monkey Don't Stop No Show Part I	12/6/71	1/10/72	11	10
	The Day I Found Myself	3/27/72	4/17/72	21	5

Hopkin, Mary
| | Temma Harbour | 3/2/70 | 3/9/70 | 36 | 3 |

Hot
| | Angel In Your Arms | 4/23/77 | 7/30/77 | 7 | 23 |

Hot Chocolate
	Emma	2/22/75	3/29/75	3	14
	You Sexy Thing	12/27/75	12/27/75	22	11
	Every 1's A Winner	2/10/79	3/10/79	20	9

Hotlegs
| | Neanderthal Man | 8/10/70 | 9/7/70 | 4 | 9 |

Houston, Thelma
| | Save The Country | 1/19/70 | 2/9/70 | 18 | 5 |
| | Don't Leave Me This Way | 3/5/77 | 4/16/77 | 4 | 17 |

Hues Corporation
| | Rock The Boat | 6/15/74 | 7/6/74 | 1 | 14 |

Humperdinck, Engelbert
| | Winter World Of Love | 12/15/69 | 1/26/70 | 13 | 9 |
| | After The Lovin' | 12/18/76 | 3/5/77 | 6 | 24 |

Hyland, Brian
| | Gypsy Woman | 10/19/70 | 11/16/70 | 2 | 10 |

Ian, Janis
| | At Seventeen | 9/6/75 | 9/27/75 | 4 | 12 |

Artist Title	Debut	Peak	Pos	Wks
Ides Of March				
Vehicle	3/23/70	4/27/70	1	12
L.A. Goodbye	3/8/71	4/5/71	5	9
Impressions				
Check Out Your Mind	6/22/70	7/13/70	23	4
also see Butler, Jerry and Brenda Lee Eager and Mayfield, Curtis				
Independents				
Leaving Me	5/21/73	6/4/73	22	4
Ingram, Luther				
My Honey And Me	12/29/69	1/26/70	19	6
(If Loving You Is Wrong) I Don't Want To Be Right	7/10/72	8/14/72	3	10
Instant Funk				
I Got My Mind Made Up (You Can Get It Girl)	4/7/79	5/12/79	26	12
Intruders				
I'll Always Love My Mama (Part 1)	7/2/73	7/2/73	29	2
Isley Brothers				
Love The One You're With	7/19/71	8/9/71	17	5
Pop That Thang	9/4/72	9/18/72	21	4
That Lady (Part 1)	9/8/73	10/13/73	14	11
Fight The Power Part 1	9/20/75	10/4/75	11	3
Take Me To The Next Phase	5/13/78	6/10/78	27	13
Jacks, Terry				
Seasons In The Sun	1/12/74	2/9/74	1	20
also see the Poppy Family				
Jackson, Jermaine				
Daddy's Home	1/29/73	3/19/73	8	9
Jackson, Joe				
Is She Really Going Out With Him	8/4/79	9/8/79	8	15
Jackson, Michael				
Got To Be There	11/8/71	12/6/71	4	12
Rockin' Robin	3/20/72	4/24/72	2	9
I Wanna Be Where You Are	6/19/72	7/24/72	11	7
Ben	9/18/72	10/16/72	1	9

Artist	Title	Debut	Peak	Pos	Wks
	Don't Stop `Til You Get Enough	9/29/79	10/27/79	7	20
	Rock With You	12/29/79	2/9/80	1	24
Jackson, Millie					
	Ask Me What You Want	5/15/72	6/12/72	16	6
Jackson 5					
	I Want You Back	11/17/69	12/15/69	2	12
	ABC	3/9/70	4/13/70	1	12
	The Love You Save	6/1/70	6/29/70	1	13
	I'll Be There	9/14/70	10/12/70	1	13
	Mama's Pearl	1/18/71	2/15/71	1	10
	Never Can Say Goodbye	3/22/71	5/10/71	2	12
	Maybe Tomorrow	7/19/71	8/16/71	7	8
	Sugar Daddy	12/13/71	1/24/72	4	12
	Little Bitty Pretty One	4/10/72	5/29/72	4	11
	Corner Of The Sky	12/4/72	12/11/72	16	4
	Dancing Machine	5/4/74	6/15/74	4	13
	I Am Love (Parts I & II)	3/8/75	4/19/75	8	13
Jacksons					
	Enjoy Yourself	1/8/77	3/5/77	12	15
	Shake Your Body (Down To The Ground)	4/7/79	5/26/79	4	22
Jaggerz					
	The Rapper	1/26/70	3/2/70	2	12
James, Rick					
	You And I	8/5/78	9/30/78	13	18
James, Tommy & the Shondells					
	She	12/8/69	12/29/69	23	6
	Gotta Get Back To You	2/9/70	3/9/70	19	6
James, Tommy					
	Draggin' The Line	6/21/71	7/26/71	1	10
	I'm Comin' Home	10/4/71	10/18/71	12	4
	Nothing To Hide	11/29/71	12/13/71	11	7
Jay & the Americans					
	Walkin' In The Rain	12/22/69	2/2/70	11	9
Jefferson					
	Baby Take Me In Your Arms	2/2/70	2/23/70	29	4

Artist Title	Debut	Peak	Pos	Wks
Jefferson Starship				
Miracles	10/25/75	11/15/75	3	15
With Your Love	8/14/76	9/25/76	8	13
Count On Me	5/13/78	6/10/78	21	12
Runaway	7/22/78	8/12/78	27	9
Jane	12/8/79	1/19/80	6	16
Jennings, Waylon				
Luckenbach, Texas (Back To The Basics Of Love)	7/16/77	8/6/77	31	5
Jethro Tull				
Living In The Past	12/18/72	1/8/73	9	7
Bungle In The Jungle	12/28/74	2/8/75	7	13
Jigsaw				
Sky High	11/22/75	12/13/75	4	17
Jo Jo Gunne				
Run Run Run	4/17/72	5/8/72	10	6
also see Ferguson, Jay and Firefall				
Joel, Billy				
Just The Way You Are	12/31/77	2/25/78	2	29
Only The Good Die Young	7/15/78	8/12/78	17	18
My Life	11/25/78	1/20/79	3	22
Big Shot	3/17/79	4/14/79	19	11
John, Elton				
Your Song	12/28/70	1/25/71	2	10
Friends	4/12/71	4/19/71	25	2
Rocket Man	6/12/72	7/10/72	8	8
Honky Cat	9/4/72	9/25/72	9	6
Crocodile Rock	1/8/73	2/5/73	1	12
Daniel	4/30/73	6/11/73	3	9
Saturday Night's Alright For Fighting	8/11/73	9/22/73	4	12
Goodbye Yellow Brick Road	10/27/73	12/22/73	1	16
Bennie And The Jets	3/9/74	4/6/74	1	15
Don't Let The Sun Go Down On Me	7/20/74	8/17/74	4	11
The Bitch Is Back	9/21/74	11/2/74	1	16

Artist	Title	Debut	Peak	Pos	Wks
	Lucy In The Sky With Diamonds	11/30/74	1/4/75	1	16
	Philadelphia Freedom	3/8/75	4/12/75	1	23
	Pinball Wizard	4/19/75	5/10/75	16	24
	Someone Saved My Life Tonight	7/26/75	8/23/75	1	18
	Island Girl	10/11/75	11/15/75	1	19
	Grow Some Funk Of Your Own	3/6/76	3/13/76	33	5
	Sorry Seems To Be The Hardest Word	12/4/76	1/15/77	12	13
	Bite Your Lip (Get Up And Dance!)	2/19/77	3/12/77	28	5
	Part-Time Love	12/23/78	1/13/79	29	8
	Mama Can't Buy You Love	7/14/79	8/25/79	22	14

John, Elton & Kiki Dee
	Don't Go Breaking My Heart	7/24/76	8/14/76	1	20

John, Robert
	The Lion Sleeps Tonight	1/31/72	2/28/72	3	12
	Sad Eyes	8/18/79	9/29/79	2	24

Johns, Sammy
	Chevy Van	4/5/75	5/10/75	5	14

Johnson, Kevin
	Rock 'N Roll (I Gave You The Best Years Of My Life)	11/17/73	11/24/73	37	2

Johnson, Michael
	Bluer Than Blue	7/15/78	8/19/78	19	11

Joli, France
	Come To Me	11/10/79	12/1/79	18	11

Jones, Davy
	Rainy Jane	6/21/71	7/12/71	14	5

Jones, Quincy
	Stuff Like That	7/1/78	7/22/78	25	13

Jones, Rickie Lee
	Chuck E.'s In Love	6/9/79	7/21/79	10	16

Jones, Tom
	Without Love (There Is Nothing)	12/22/69	2/2/70	7	10
	Daughter 0f Darkness	4/20/70	6/8/70	2	12

Artist	Title	Debut	Peak	Pos	Wks
	I (Who Have Nothing)	8/10/70	9/21/70	4	10
	Can't Stop Loving You	11/30/70	12/14/70	20	4
	She's A Lady	1/25/71	4/5/71	1	14
	Puppet Man	5/10/71	6/7/71	22	5
	Say You'll Stay Until Tomorrow	2/19/77	4/16/77	19	13

Joplin, Janis

	Me And Bobby McGee	2/8/71	3/8/71	2	10

Journey

	Lovin', Touchin', Squeezin'	9/22/79	11/10/79	2	25

Kansas

	Carry On Wayward Son	1/22/77	3/19/77	2	20
	Point Of Know Return	12/3/77	1/28/78	11	14
	Dust In The Wind	3/18/78	5/13/78	6	22

KC & the Sunshine Band

	Get Down Tonight	9/6/75	9/27/75	1	21
	That's The Way (I Like It)	11/15/75	12/6/75	1	24
	(Shake, Shake, Shake) Shake Your Booty	7/31/76	9/18/76	3	17
	I Like To Do It	1/8/77	1/22/77	36	4
	I'm Your Boogie Man	4/23/77	6/11/77	2	20
	Keep It Comin' Love	9/3/77	10/15/77	2	18
	Please Don't Go	11/17/79	1/12/80	3	21

Kendalls

	Heaven's Just A Sin Away	11/26/77	12/10/77	32	6

Kendricks, Eddie

	Keep On Truckin' (Part 1)	9/22/73	10/27/73	6	14
	Boogie Down	2/2/74	3/2/74	7	8

also see the Temptations

Khan, Chaka

	I'm Every Woman	11/25/78	12/30/78	23	13

also see Rufus

Kim, Andy

	Be My Baby	11/16/70	12/14/70	7	8
	Rock Me Gently	8/24/74	9/21/74	1	13

Artist	Title	Debut	Peak	Pos	Wks

King, B.B.
| | The Thrill Is Gone | 1/26/70 | 2/16/70 | 30 | 4 |
| | Never Make A Move Too Soon | 8/26/78 | 9/23/78 | 31 | 10 |

King, Carole
	It's Too Late	5/24/71	6/21/71	1	14
	/I Feel The Earth Move	8/9/71	8/9/71	15	3
	So Far Away	9/6/71	10/11/71	10	8
	/Smackwater Jack	9/20/71	10/11/71	10	6
	Sweet Seasons	1/10/72	2/28/72	8	14
	Believe In Humanity	7/16/73	9/1/73	25	7
	Jazzman	10/12/74	11/9/74	3	14

King, Evelyn "Champagne"
| | Shame | 5/27/78 | 7/1/78 | 17 | 27 |
| | I Don't Know If It's Right | 12/30/78 | 2/17/79 | 23 | 14 |

King Harvest
| | Dancing In The Moonlight | 1/8/73 | 2/5/73 | 12 | 10 |

Kinks
| | Lola | 9/21/70 | 10/19/70 | 4 | 9 |

Kiss
	Rock And Roll All Nite	12/27/75	1/31/76	6	17
	Beth	9/25/76	12/11/76	3	24
	Hard Luck Woman	1/22/77	3/12/77	7	14
	Calling Dr. Love	4/9/77	5/21/77	5	16
	Christine Sixteen	7/30/77	8/20/77	26	8
	I Was Made For Lovin' You	6/30/79	8/4/79	15	18

Kissoon, Mac & Katie
| | Chirpy Chirpy Cheep Cheep | 9/6/71 | 9/27/71 | 12 | 6 |

Knack
| | My Sharona | 7/28/79 | 8/18/79 | 1 | 27 |
| | Good Girls Don't | 9/29/79 | 11/3/79 | 7 | 18 |

Knight, Frederick
| | I've Been Lonely For So Long | 6/5/72 | 6/12/72 | 26 | 2 |

Knight, Gladys & the Pips
| | You Need Love Like I Do (Don't You) | 4/6/70 | 4/13/70 | 31 | 4 |

Artist	Title	Debut	Peak	Pos	Wks
	If I Were Your Woman	12/21/70	1/25/71	4	10
	I Don't Want To Do Wrong	6/21/71	7/12/71	18	5
	Neither One Of Us (Wants To Be The First To Say Goodbye)	2/26/73	4/2/73	4	9
	Daddy Could Swear, I Declare	6/11/73	6/18/73	23	5
	Midnight Train To Georgia	9/22/73	11/17/73	6	14
	I've Got To Use My Imagination	12/22/73	2/23/74	11	13
	Best Thing That Ever Happened To Me	4/13/74	5/11/74	8	10
	On And On	8/3/74	8/31/74	13	5

Knight, Jean
	Mr. Big Stuff	6/14/71	7/12/71	4	8
	You Think You're Hot Stuff	10/11/71	11/1/71	19	4

Kool & the Gang
	Jungle Boogie	3/16/74	3/30/74	12	4
	Ladies Night	10/27/79	12/1/79	8	25

Kraftwerk
	Autobahn	5/3/75	5/17/75	12	4

Labelle
	Lady Marmalade	3/15/75	4/5/75	2	16

Landecker, John Records
	Press My Conference	3/9/74	3/9/74	23	2

Larson, Nicolette
	Lotta Love	1/20/79	2/17/79	12	14

LaSalle, Denise
	Trapped By A Thing Called Love	10/18/71	11/8/71	12	6

Lawrence, Vicki
	The Night The Lights Went Out In Georgia	3/26/73	4/9/73	1	10

Led Zeppelin
	Whole Lotta Love	11/24/69	1/5/70	2	11
	Immigrant Song	12/7/70	1/18/71	3	10
	Black Dog	12/27/71	1/31/72	4	10
	Over The Hills And Far Away	7/16/73	7/23/73	22	2
	D'yer Mak'er	11/3/73	12/8/73	6	12
	All Of My Love	10/13/79	10/20/79	47	2

Artist Title	Debut	Peak	Pos	Wks
Lennon, John				
Instant Karma (We All Shine On)	2/23/70	3/16/70	2	11
Power To The People	4/5/71	5/3/71	9	7
Imagine	10/18/71	11/15/71	2	9
Mind Games	11/10/73	12/15/73	6	13
Whatever Gets You Thru The Night	10/19/74	11/23/74	8	13
also see the Beatles				
Lettermen				
Traces/Memories Medley	1/5/70	1/19/70	33	5
Lightfoot, Gordon				
If You Could Read My Mind	1/18/71	2/22/71	2	10
Sundown	5/25/74	6/22/74	1	14
The Wreck Of The Edmund Fitzgerald	9/11/76	10/30/76	3	20
Lighthouse				
One Fine Morning	9/20/71	10/18/71	10	7
Sunny Days	11/20/72	12/4/72	26	3
Lindsay, Mark				
Arizona	1/19/70	2/16/70	7	9
Silver Bird	7/13/70	8/3/70	21	5
also see the Raiders				
Little River Band				
It's A Long Way There	10/23/76	11/20/76	31	6
Help Is On Its Way	10/1/77	12/10/77	19	14
Reminiscing	9/30/78	11/4/78	6	16
Lady	3/3/79	5/5/79	7	22
Lonesome Loser	8/25/79	10/27/79	6	21
Cool Change	12/22/79	1/26/80	24	11
Little Sister				
You're The One-Part I	3/30/70	4/13/70	34	3
Somebody's Watching You	1/4/71	1/4/71	31	1
Lobo				
Me And You And A Dog Named Boo	3/22/71	4/26/71	3	9
I'm The Only One	6/7/71	7/19/71	11	8
I'd Love You To Want Me	10/23/72	11/27/72	2	8

Artist	Title	Debut	Peak	Pos	Wks
	Don't Expect Me To Be Your Friend	1/22/73	2/19/73	4	8
	It Sure Took A Long, Long Time	5/7/73	5/14/73	20	2
	How Can I Tell Her	7/30/73	9/1/73	26	8
Loggins, Dave					
	Please Come To Boston	8/24/74	9/7/74	21	5
Loggins & Messina					
	Your Mama Don't Dance	12/4/72	1/29/73	4	12
	Thinking Of You	4/30/73	5/28/73	15	6
Loggins, Kenny					
	Whenever I Call You "Friend"	10/7/78	12/2/78	8	17
also see Poco					
Looking Glass					
	Brandy (You're A Fine Girl)	7/3/72	8/28/72	1	14
	Jimmy Loves Mary-Anne	9/15/73	10/13/73	2	11
Love Unlimited					
	Walkin' In The Rain With The One I Love	5/22/72	6/12/72	10	7
Love Unlimited Orchestra					
	Love's Theme	12/15/73	2/16/74	4	15
also see White, Barry					
Lowe, Nick					
	Cruel To Be Kind	9/22/79	10/20/79	15	12
L.T.D.					
	Love Ballad	11/6/76	12/4/76	26	7
	(Every Time I Turn Around) Back In Love Again	11/12/77	12/24/77	22	13
Lulu					
	Oh Me, Oh My (I'm A Fool For You Baby)	2/2/70	3/2/70	19	5
	Hum A Song (From Your Heart)	4/27/70	5/11/70	28	3
Lynn, Cheryl					
	Got To Be Real	12/2/78	2/17/79	13	21
	Star Love	5/5/79	6/2/79	22	10
Lynyrd Skynyrd					
	Sweet Home Alabama	9/21/74	10/19/74	3	13
	Free Bird	12/4/76	1/8/77	10	12
	What's Your Name	1/14/78	2/25/78	15	15

Artist	Title	Debut	Peak	Pos	Wks
M					
	Pop Muzik	9/29/79	12/22/79	3	23
MacGregor, Byron					
	Americans	1/5/74	2/2/74	5	8
MacGregor, Mary					
	Torn Between Two Lovers	12/25/76	2/26/77	1	23
Maggard, Cledus & the Citizen's Band					
	The White Knight	1/24/76	2/21/76	20	12
Magic Lanterns					
	Country Woman	6/12/72	6/26/72	22	3
Main Ingredient					
	Everybody Plays The Fool	9/4/72	10/23/72	1	11
	Just Don't Want To Be Lonely	4/20/74	5/4/74	14	4
Malo					
	Suavecito	4/10/72	5/15/72	5	9
Manchester, Melissa					
	Midnight Blue	7/19/75	8/23/75	5	14
	Don't Cry Out Loud	3/3/79	3/31/79	13	14
Mancini, Henry					
	Theme From Love Story	2/1/71	3/1/71	3	8
Mangione, Chuck					
	Feels So Good	5/27/78	6/24/78	4	18
Manhattans					
	There's No Me Without You	7/2/73	7/9/73	24	2
	Kiss And Say Goodbye	7/10/76	8/28/76	23	9
Manilow, Barry					
	Mandy	1/4/75	1/25/75	1	16
	It's A Miracle	4/19/75	5/24/75	1	16
	Could It Be Magic	8/9/75	9/13/75	6	14
	I Write The Songs	12/6/75	1/31/76	1	24
	Tryin' To Get The Feeling Again	4/10/76	5/22/76	8	13
	This One's For You	9/18/76	11/6/76	7	18

Artist	Title	Debut	Peak	Pos	Wks
	Weekend In New England	12/11/76	1/29/77	1	21
	Looks Like We Made It	5/14/77	7/16/77	3	18
	Daybreak	10/15/77	11/19/77	8	15
	Can't Smile Without You	2/18/78	4/15/78	4	25
	Copacabana (At The Copa)	7/1/78	7/29/78	9	19
	Ready To Take A Chance Again	10/14/78	12/2/78	10	16
	Somewhere In The Night	2/3/79	3/3/79	20	9
	Ships	10/13/79	12/8/79	13	17

Mann's, Manfred, Earth Band
| | Blinded By The Light | 12/4/76 | 1/1/77 | 1 | 20 |

Marmalade
| | Reflections Of My Life | 3/23/70 | 5/11/70 | 2 | 14 |

Marshall Tucker Band
| | Heard It In A Love Song | 5/21/77 | 6/25/77 | 22 | 11 |

Martin, Bobbi
| | For The Love Of Him | 3/30/70 | 5/11/70 | 8 | 12 |

Martin, Steve & the Toot Uncommons
| | King Tut | 6/10/78 | 7/22/78 | 1 | 21 |

Martino, Al
| | I Started Loving You Again | 12/29/69 | 1/5/70 | 38 | 2 |

Mason, Barbara
| | Give Me Your Love | 2/12/73 | 2/19/73 | 24 | 3 |

Mason, Dave
| | We Just Disagree | 10/29/77 | 12/10/77 | 25 | 9 |

Mass Production
| | Firecracker | 9/29/79 | 10/20/79 | 32 | 7 |

Mathis, Johnny & Deniece Williams
| | Too Much, Too Little, Too Late | 4/1/78 | 5/27/78 | 1 | 22 |

also see Williams, Deniece

Matthews, Ian
| | Shake It | 1/20/79 | 2/17/79 | 17 | 13 |

Artist Title	Debut	Peak	Pos	Wks
Mayfield, Curtis				
Freddie's Dead (Theme From "Superfly")	10/16/72	11/6/72	4	8
Superfly	12/11/72	1/22/73	7	10
also see the Impressions				
McCall, C.W.				
Convoy	12/13/75	12/27/75	1	22
McCann, Peter				
Do You Wanna Make Love	6/4/77	8/6/77	4	20
McCartney, Paul				
Another Day	3/15/71	4/5/71	3	7
My Love	5/14/73	6/4/73	1	10
McCartney, Paul & Linda				
Uncle Albert/Admiral Halsey	8/2/71	8/23/71	3	11
McCartney, Paul & Wings				
Helen Wheels	11/24/73	1/5/74	13	11
Jet	3/2/74	4/20/74	10	12
Band On The Run	5/11/74	6/15/74	1	15
Junior's Farm	11/23/74	12/21/74	7	13
Wings				
Live And Let Die	7/2/73	9/1/73	1	14
Listen To What The Man Said	6/28/75	8/9/75	1	17
Venus And Mars Rock Show	12/27/75	12/27/75	23	4
Silly Love Songs	4/24/76	5/29/76	1	22
Let 'Em In	7/17/76	8/28/76	2	16
Maybe I'm Amazed	2/26/77	4/2/77	15	10
Girls' School	12/24/77	1/14/78	27	8
With A Little Luck	4/22/78	6/17/78	4	19
Goodnight Tonight	3/24/79	5/19/79	9	20
Getting Closer	6/16/79	7/28/79	20	13
also see the Beatles				
McCoo, Marilyn & Billy Davis, Jr.				
You Don't Have To Be A Star (To Be In My Show)	11/13/76	12/25/76	6	18
Your Love	4/23/77	5/14/77	27	6
also see the Fifth Dimension				

Artist Title	Debut	Peak	Pos	Wks
McCoy, Van with the Soul City Symphony				
The Hustle	6/21/75	7/12/75	4	19
McCrae, George				
Rock Your Baby	7/6/74	8/3/74	1	11
McCrae, Gwen				
Rockin' Chair	7/12/75	8/23/75	10	8
McDowell, Ronnie				
The King Is Gone	9/24/77	10/29/77	10	10
McFadden & Whitehead				
Ain't No Stoppin' Us Now	6/9/79	7/7/79	20	14
McGovern, Maureen				
The Morning After	7/9/73	8/11/73	2	13
McGuinness Flint				
When I'm Dead And Gone	1/11/71	2/1/71	20	5
McLean, Don				
American Pie—Parts I & II	12/6/71	1/3/72	1	16
Castles In The Air	4/3/72	5/8/72	14	8
Dreidel	1/29/73	2/5/73	21	2
McNamara, Robin				
Lay A Little Lovin' On Me	6/22/70	8/3/70	6	11
Mead, Sister Janet				
The Lord's Prayer	3/23/74	4/27/74	2	9
Meat Loaf				
Two Out Of Three Ain't Bad	7/22/78	9/2/78	11	19
Meco				
Star Wars Theme/Cantina Band	9/10/77	10/22/77	2	22
Mel & Tim				
Starting All Over Again	10/2/72	10/16/72	19	6
Melanie				
Lay Down (Candles In The Rain)	5/11/70	6/22/70	5	14
Peace Will Come (According To Plan)	8/24/70	9/14/70	28	4
Brand New Key	11/22/71	12/20/71	1	12

Artist	Title	Debut	Peak	Pos	Wks
	The Nickel Song	2/7/72	3/6/72	18	5
	Ring The Living Bell	2/14/72	3/6/72	20	4

Melvin, Harold & the Blue Notes

	If You Don't Know Me By Now	11/13/72	12/4/72	7	10
	The Love I Lost (Part 1)	11/17/73	12/8/73	21	8

also see Pendergrass, Teddy

MFSB featuring the Three Degrees

	TSOP (The Sound Of Philadelphia)	4/6/74	5/11/74	5	12

also see the Three Degrees

Michaels, Lee

	Do You Know What I Mean	9/6/71	10/11/71	2	11

Midler, Bette

	Do You Want To Dance	2/5/73	3/12/73	12	6
	Boogie Woogie Bugle Boy	6/11/73	7/16/73	2	10

Miller, Steve

	The Joker	11/24/73	12/29/73	1	14
	Take The Money And Run	5/29/76	7/24/76	15	14
	Rock'n Me	9/25/76	11/6/76	3	18
	Fly Like An Eagle	1/1/77	3/5/77	2	23
	Jet Airliner	5/21/77	7/2/77	7	14
	Jungle Love	9/3/77	10/15/77	23	11
	Swingtown	11/19/77	12/10/77	28	8

also see Scaggs, Boz

Mills, Frank

	Music Box Dancer	3/24/79	4/21/79	2	17

Miracles, Smokey Robinson & the

	The Tears Of A Clown	10/26/70	11/23/70	1	11
	I Don't Blame You At All	4/5/71	4/26/71	12	5
	Crazy About The La La La	8/2/71	8/2/71	32	1

Miracles

	Love Machine (Part 1)	1/31/76	2/28/76	16	13

Mitchell, Joni

	You Turn Me On, I'm A Radio	1/29/73	2/5/73	19	2
	Help Me	5/18/74	6/29/74	6	11

Artist	Title	Debut	Peak	Pos	Wks
Mocedades					
	Eres Tu (Touch The Wind)	3/23/74	4/13/74	5	7
Moments					
	Love On A Two-Way Street	5/4/70	6/15/70	5	11
Moody Blues					
	Question	5/11/70	6/22/70	13	10
	The Story In Your Eyes	8/30/71	9/13/71	14	6
	Isn't Life Strange	5/22/72	6/5/72	16	4
	Nights In White Satin	9/18/72	10/30/72	1	11
	I'm Just A Singer (In A Rock And Roll Band)	2/12/73	3/19/73	7	8
Moore, Dorothy					
	Misty Blue	5/1/76	6/26/76	7	16
Moore, Jackie					
	Sweet Charlie Babe	9/1/73	9/29/73	8	8
Morrison, Van					
	Come Running	4/13/70	4/20/70	36	2
	Domino	11/23/70	1/4/71	3	11
	Blue Money	2/15/71	3/15/71	7	8
	Wild Night	11/8/71	11/29/71	6	7
Mountain					
	Mississippi Queen	6/15/70	8/3/70	12	10
Mouth & MacNeal					
	How Do You Do	6/12/72	8/14/72	6	11
Muldaur, Maria					
	Midnight At The Oasis	5/11/74	6/15/74	7	10
Mungo Jerry					
	In The Summertime	7/20/70	8/31/70	4	11
Murphey, Michael					
	Wildfire	6/7/75	6/28/75	1	16
Murphy, Walter & the Big Apple Band					
	A Fifth Of Beethoven	8/7/76	9/25/76	4	26

Artist Title	Debut	Peak	Pos	Wks
Murray, Anne				
Snowbird	8/31/70	9/14/70	20	6
Danny's Song	2/26/73	4/16/73	5	10
Love Song	2/23/74	3/16/74	5	9
You Won't See Me	6/22/74	7/20/74	5	10
You Needed Me	9/23/78	11/25/78	4	25
I Just Fall In Love Again	4/21/79	5/5/79	33	7
Shadows In The Moonlight	8/4/79	8/25/79	34	8
Broken Hearted Me	11/17/79	12/15/79	24	10
Nash, Johnny				
Cupid	12/22/69	12/29/69	35	3
I Can See Clearly Now	10/16/72	11/13/72	1	11
Stir It Up	3/19/73	4/23/73	10	8
Naughton, David				
Makin' It	5/12/79	6/30/79	2	25
Nazareth				
Love Hurts	2/7/76	4/3/76	5	16
Neely, Sam				
Loving You Just Crossed My Mind	10/16/72	10/30/72	26	3
Neighborhood				
Big Yellow Taxi	7/20/70	8/17/70	11	7
Nelson, Rick & the Stone Canyon Band				
She Belongs To Me	1/5/70	1/19/70	31	3
Garden Party	9/25/72	11/6/72	2	9
Nero, Peter				
Theme From "Summer Of '42"	11/22/71	12/13/71	20	5
Nesmith, Michael & the First National Band				
Joanne	9/28/70	10/12/70	13	5

Artist Title	Debut	Peak	Pos	Wks
New Colony Six				
Barbara, I Love You	12/8/69	1/12/70	13	8
People And Me	4/27/70	5/11/70	32	4
New Seekers				
Look What They've Done To My Song Ma	10/4/70	10/19/70	7	7
I'd Like To Teach The World To Sing (In Perfect Harmony)	11/29/71	1/17/72	9	12
Pinball Wizard/See Me, Feel Me	4/23/73	4/23/73	25	1
New York City				
I'm Doin' Fine Now	5/7/73	6/18/73	15	10
Newman, Randy				
Short People	12/24/77	1/28/78	2	19
Newton, Wayne				
Daddy Don't You Walk So Fast	6/19/72	8/7/72	3	11
Newton-John, Olivia				
If Not For You	5/31/71	6/28/71	2	7
Let Me Be There	12/15/73	1/12/74	9	12
If You Love Me (Let Me Know)	6/29/74	7/6/74	7	6
I Honestly Love You	9/14/74	10/5/74	1	16
Have You Never Been Mellow	1/25/75	3/15/75	1	22
Please Mr. Please	6/28/75	8/2/75	4	14
Come On Over	5/1/76	5/22/76	25	7
Don't Stop Believin'	9/4/76	9/25/76	27	6
Sam	3/12/77	4/16/77	30	7
Hopelessly Devoted To You	8/12/78	9/23/78	7	16
A Little More Love	1/13/79	2/17/79	6	18
Deeper Than The Night	5/5/79	6/23/79	29	12

also see Travolta, John & Olivia Newton-John

Artist Title	Debut	Peak	Pos	Wks
Nicholas, Paul				
Heaven On The 7th Floor	10/22/77	12/31/77	4	21
Night				
Hot Summer Nights	8/11/79	9/29/79	17	13
Nightingale, Maxine				
Right Back Where We Started From	3/20/76	5/1/76	2	15
Lead Me On	8/18/79	9/22/79	11	16

Artist Title	Debut	Peak	Pos	Wks
Nilsson				
Without You	1/24/72	2/28/72	1	13
Coconut	7/24/72	8/28/72	9	7
Nitty Gritty Dirt Band				
Mr. Bojangles	2/8/71	3/1/71	11	6
Nolan, Kenny				
I Like Dreamin'	2/5/77	4/30/77	7	18
Nugent, Ted				
Cat Scratch Fever	9/3/77	10/8/77	31	8
Ocean				
Put Your Hand In The Hand	3/22/71	5/3/71	2	10
Ocean, Billy				
Love Really Hurts Without You	5/29/76	6/12/76	38	3
O'Day, Alan				
Undercover Angel	5/28/77	7/16/77	1	23
Odyssey				
Native New Yorker	1/21/78	3/4/78	18	13
Ohio Players				
Skin Tight	10/26/74	11/9/74	13	3
Fire	2/15/75	3/22/75	4	14
Love Rollercoaster	12/27/75	1/24/76	4	19
O'Jays				
Back Stabbers	8/14/72	9/18/72	2	10
Love Train	2/5/73	3/26/73	1	11
For The Love Of Money	6/8/74	6/22/74	6	6
I Love Music (Part 1)	12/27/75	1/31/76	12	14
Use Ta Be My Girl	5/13/78	7/8/78	8	20
O'Keefe, Danny				
Good Time Charlie's Got The Blues	10/2/72	11/6/72	9	8
Oldfield, Mike				
Tubular Bells	3/30/74	4/20/74	5	12
Olsson, Nigel				
Dancin' Shoes	3/31/79	3/31/79	44	1

Artist Title	Debut	Peak	Pos	Wks
100 Proof Aged In Soul				
Somebody's Been Sleeping	10/4/70	11/2/70	6	9
Original Caste				
One Tin Soldier	2/9/70	2/16/70	36	2
Originals				
The Bells	3/23/70	4/13/70	23	6
Orleans				
Dance With Me	9/27/75	10/25/75	2	13
Still The One	8/21/76	10/16/76	6	18
Osmond, Donny				
Sweet And Innocent	4/12/71	5/24/71	2	10
Go Away Little Girl	8/9/71	9/13/71	1	13
Hey Girl	12/6/71	12/27/71	4	11
Puppy Love	3/13/72	3/27/72	3	8
Too Young	7/3/72	7/17/72	8	4
Why	9/11/72	10/9/72	16	7
Twelfth Of Never, The	4/9/73	5/21/73	6	8
Young Love	8/25/73	9/29/73	20	7
/A Million To One	8/25/73	9/29/73	20	7
Are You Lonesome Tonight	1/5/74	1/19/74	35	3
Osmond, Donny & Marie				
I'm Leaving It (All) Up To You	8/10/74	9/14/74	5	11
Morning Side Of The Mountain	12/28/74	2/1/75	5	12
Deep Purple	3/13/76	4/24/76	7	16
Osmond, Marie				
Paper Roses	9/29/73	11/17/73	4	14
Osmonds				
One Bad Apple	1/11/71	2/1/71	1	9
Double Lovin'	5/3/71	6/14/71	5	9
Yo-Yo	9/20/71	10/25/71	1	11
Down By The Lazy River	1/17/72	2/28/72	2	16
Hold Her Tight	7/17/72	8/7/72	11	5
Crazy Horses	11/6/72	12/4/72	18	5
Let Me In	9/15/73	10/20/73	12	12
Love Me For A Reason	9/28/74	11/9/74	7	14

Artist	Title	Debut	Peak	Pos	Wks
O'Sullivan, Gilbert					
	Alone Again (Naturally)	7/3/72	7/31/72	1	13
	Clair	11/13/72	12/25/72	2	13
	Out Of The Question	4/16/73	5/7/73	19	4
	Get Down	6/25/73	7/30/73	2	11
	Ooh Baby	10/6/73	11/24/73	12	13
Ozark Mountain Daredevils					
	Jackie Blue	4/5/75	5/10/75	1	16
Pablo Cruise					
	Whatcha Gonna Do	7/2/77	8/27/77	6	15
	Love Will Find A Way	8/5/78	9/16/78	6	20
Pacific Gas & Electric					
	Are You Ready	6/22/70	7/27/70	15	9
Palmer, Robert					
	Bad Case Of Loving You (Doctor, Doctor)	9/22/79	10/20/79	11	15
Paper Lace					
	The Night Chicago Died	7/27/74	8/10/74	1	15
Parks, Michael					
	Long Lonesome Highway	3/16/70	4/13/70	9	8
Parliament					
	Tear The Roof Off The Sucker (Give Up The Funk)	6/19/76	7/17/76	25	8
	Flash Light	3/4/78	5/20/78	3	23
	Aqua Boogie (A Psychoalphadiscobetabioaquadoloop)	1/20/79	2/24/79	21	12
Parsons, Alan					
	I Wouldn't Want To Be Like You	10/1/77	11/5/77	21	10
Parton, Dolly					
	Here You Come Again	11/26/77	1/14/78	3	17
Partridge Family					
	I Think I Love You	10/19/70	11/2/70	1	12
	Doesn't Somebody Want To Be Wanted	2/1/71	3/8/71	1	11
	I'll Meet You Halfway	4/12/71	6/7/71	5	11
	I Woke Up In Love This Morning	8/9/71	9/20/71	3	10
	It's One Of Those Nights (Yes Love)	12/13/71	1/10/72	7	9

Artist	Title	Debut	Peak	Pos	Wks
	Breaking Up Is Hard To Do	7/31/72	8/7/72	22	2
also see Cassidy, David					
Patterson, Kellee					
	If It Don't Fit, Don't Force It	3/4/78	3/4/78	45	2
Paul, Billy					
	Me And Mrs. Jones	11/27/72	12/25/72	1	12
Payne, Freda					
	Band Of Gold	6/1/70	7/20/70	2	14
	Deeper & Deeper	9/21/70	11/2/70	7	11
	Bring The Boys Home	6/7/71	7/5/71	17	6
Peaches & Herb					
	Shake Your Groove Thing	2/10/79	3/24/79	4	24
	Reunited	3/31/79	5/19/79	1	21
Pendergrass, Teddy					
	Close The Door	7/1/78	7/29/78	19	15
also see Melvin, Harold & the Blue Notes					
Peter, Paul & Mary					
	Leaving On A Jet Plane	10/13/69	12/1/69	4	15
also see Stookey, Paul					
Petty, Tom & the Heartbreakers					
	Don't Do Me Like That	12/22/79	2/9/80	6	21
Pickett, Bobby "Boris" & the Crypt-Kickers					
	Monster Mash	6/25/73	7/9/73	3	9
Pickett, Wilson					
	Sugar, Sugar	6/8/70	7/13/70	19	6
	Engine Number 9	11/16/70	11/16/70	26	1
	Don't Let The Green Grass Fool You	3/1/71	3/15/71	21	3
	Don't Knock My Love—Pt. 1	5/17/71	6/21/71	7	8
	Fire And Water	1/17/72	1/17/72	31	1
Pilot					
	Magic	6/14/75	6/28/75	2	15
Pink Floyd					
	Money	6/4/73	7/16/73	10	9

Artist Title	Debut	Peak	Pos	Wks
Pipkins				
Gimme Dat Ding	5/18/70	7/6/70	7	10
also see the Brotherhood of Man, Edison Lighthouse, First Class and White Plains				
Place, Mary Kay as Loretta Haggers				
Baby Boy	11/13/76	12/18/76	24	8
Player				
Baby Come Back	12/3/77	2/4/78	4	24
P-Nut Gallery				
Do You Know What Time It Is	5/24/71	6/21/71	8	6
Poco				
Crazy Love	3/24/79	4/14/79	17	13
Heart Of The Night	7/21/79	8/4/79	33	7
also see the Eagles and Loggins & Messina				
Pointer, Bonnie				
Heaven Must Have Sent You	10/13/79	10/27/79	33	8
Pointer Sisters				
Yes We Can Can	9/22/73	11/3/73	14	11
Fire	2/3/79	3/31/79	2	21
Poppy Family featuring Susan Jacks				
Which Way You Goin' Billy	3/23/70	5/11/70	5	15
That's Where I Went Wrong	9/7/70	10/12/70	8	9
also see Jacks, Terry				
Post, Mike				
The Rockford Files	8/16/75	8/30/75	12	5
Pratt & McClain				
Happy Days	5/1/76	6/5/76	3	13
Presidents				
5-10-15-20 (25-30 Years Of Love)	11/9/70	11/30/70	11	6
Presley, Elvis				
Don't Cry Daddy	11/24/69	1/12/70	4	11
Kentucky Rain	2/9/70	3/16/70	12	9
The Wonder Of You	5/25/70	7/6/70	9	9
You Don't Have To Say You Love Me	11/2/70	11/30/70	7	7
I Really Don't Want To Know	1/11/71	2/8/71	7	7

Artist	Title	Debut	Peak	Pos	Wks
	Where Did They Go, Lord	3/29/71	3/29/71	31	1
	Burning Love	8/14/72	10/30/72	2	14
	Separate Ways	1/22/73	1/22/73	21	2
	Steamroller Blues	5/14/73	6/4/73	16	6
	/Fool	6/11/73	6/11/73	17	2
	Raised On Rock	9/29/73	10/27/73	30	6
	My Way	12/10/77	1/7/78	18	10
	Softly As I Leave You	4/22/78	5/13/78	35	7

Preston, Billy
	Outa-Space	5/15/72	7/3/72	2	11
	Will It Go Round In Circles	6/4/73	7/9/73	1	10
	Space Race	10/27/73	12/15/73	12	13
	Nothing From Nothing	9/14/74	10/12/74	3	13

Price, Ray
	For The Good Times	12/21/70	1/4/71	14	4

Procol Harum
	Conquistador	7/3/72	7/31/72	12	6

Q
	Dancin' Man	4/30/77	5/28/77	29	7

Quatro, Suzi & Chris Norman
	Stumblin' In	4/7/79	5/19/79	11	18

Queen
	Killer Queen	4/26/75	5/31/75	1	19
	Bohemian Rhapsody	2/21/76	4/3/76	1	22
	You're My Best Friend	6/12/76	8/7/76	4	16
	Somebody To Love	1/1/77	1/29/77	18	10
	We Are The Champions	12/10/77	1/14/78	1	23
	/We Will Rock You	12/24/77	1/14/78	1	21
	Bicycle Race	12/16/78	1/20/79	20	11
	/Fat Bottomed Girls	12/16/78	1/20/79	20	11

Rafferty, Gerry
	Baker Street	6/10/78	7/8/78	4	22
	Right Down The Line	10/14/78	11/25/78	19	12

also see Stealers Wheel

Artist	Title	Debut	Peak	Pos	Wks
Raiders					
	Indian Reservation (The Lament Of The Cherokee Reservation Indian)	5/31/71	7/5/71	5	10
	Birds Of A Feather	9/27/71	10/18/71	15	7
also see Lindsay, Mark					
Ram Jam					
	Black Betty	7/9/77	9/24/77	2	20
Rare Earth					
	Get Ready	5/4/70	6/15/70	1	11
	(I Know) I'm Losing You	8/17/70	9/28/70	5	10
	Born To Wander	12/28/70	2/8/71	2	11
	I Just Want To Celebrate	7/26/71	8/30/71	8	10
	Hey Big Brother	12/13/71	1/17/72	13	10
Raspberries					
	Go All The Way	8/28/72	10/9/72	3	10
	I Wanna Be With You	12/4/72	1/15/73	16	9
	Let's Pretend	6/4/73	6/18/73	21	4
also see Carmen, Eric					
Rawls, Lou					
	A Natural Man	11/15/71	12/6/71	16	6
	You'll Never Find Another Love Like Mine	6/26/76	8/28/76	4	18
	Lady Love	3/4/78	4/22/78	19	14
Raydio					
	Jack And Jill	2/4/78	5/13/78	3	25
	You Can't Change That	7/14/79	9/8/79	10	16
Rea, Chris					
	Fool (If You Think It's Over)	9/23/78	10/14/78	26	10
Redbone					
	Come And Get Your Love	3/30/74	5/4/74	2	13
Reddy, Helen					
	I Don't Know How To Love Him	5/17/71	6/14/71	6	6
	I Am Woman	10/23/72	12/11/72	1	14
	Peaceful	4/2/73	4/23/73	13	7
	Delta Dawn	7/23/73	9/15/73	3	12
	Leave Me Alone (Ruby Red Dress)	11/3/73	12/29/73	4	15

Artist	Title	Debut	Peak	Pos	Wks
	Keep On Singing	4/27/74	5/4/74	17	2
	Angie Baby	11/16/74	12/14/74	4	15
	Ain't No Way To Treat A Lady	10/11/75	10/25/75	11	5
	You're My World	7/9/77	9/3/77	4	17
Redeye					
	Games	12/7/70	1/25/71	12	6
Reed, Jerry					
	Amos Moses	1/25/71	3/1/71	2	10
	When You're Hot, You're Hot	5/31/71	6/28/71	10	6
Reed, Lou					
	Walk On The Wild Side	6/4/73	6/11/73	19	2
Reunion					
	Life Is A Rock (But The Radio Rolled Me)	10/12/74	11/30/74	1	17
Rhythm Heritage					
	Theme From S.W.A.T.	1/31/76	2/28/76	3	20
	Baretta's Theme ('Keep Your Eye On The Sparrow')	5/15/76	6/26/76	21	9
Rich, Charlie					
	Behind Closed Doors	7/9/73	7/30/73	22	3
	The Most Beautiful Girl	12/1/73	2/2/74	1	16
Richard, Cliff					
	Devil Woman	8/21/76	10/9/76	2	19
	We Don't Talk Anymore	12/8/79	2/9/80	4	17
Righteous Brothers					
	Rock And Roll Heaven	7/6/74	7/27/74	10	5
Rios, Miguel					
	A Song Of Joy	6/8/70	7/13/70	9	10
Riperton, Minnie					
	Lovin' You	3/22/75	4/26/75	2	13
Rivers, Johnny					
	Rockin' Pneumonia—Boogie Woogie Flu	10/30/72	1/15/73	5	15
	Blue Suede Shoes	4/30/73	5/7/73	23	2
	Swayin' To The Music (Slow Dancin')	8/20/77	10/29/77	7	18

Artist Title	Debut	Peak	Pos	Wks
Roberts, Austin				
Something's Wrong With Me	11/20/72	12/25/72	10	7
Rocky	10/18/75	11/15/75	8	15
Robinson, Vicki Sue				
Turn The Beat Around	7/31/76	8/21/76	25	8
Roe, Tommy				
Jam Up Jelly Tight	11/17/69	1/5/70	5	13
Stir It Up And Serve It	2/23/70	3/23/70	21	6
Pearl	7/13/70	8/3/70	25	4
We Can Make Music	9/14/70	10/4/70	16	6
Stagger Lee	8/23/71	9/13/71	12	7
Rogers, Kenny & the First Edition				
Something's Burning	3/16/70	4/27/70	4	11
Rogers, Kenny				
Lucille	5/7/77	6/18/77	11	13
She Believes In Me	6/9/79	8/4/79	7	27
You Decorated My Life	10/20/79	11/17/79	14	16
Coward Of The County	12/15/79	1/26/80	2	22
Rolling Stones				
Brown Sugar	4/19/71	5/31/71	1	11
Tumbling Dice	5/1/72	6/12/72	4	10
Happy	7/31/72	8/21/72	17	4
You Can't Always Get What You Want	5/21/73	5/21/73	25	2
Angie	9/22/73	10/27/73	2	12
Doo Doo Doo Doo Doo (Heartbreaker)	1/12/74	2/23/74	13	8
It's Only Rock 'N Roll (But I Like It)	8/3/74	9/21/74	14	3
Fool To Cry	5/15/76	6/12/76	16	9
Miss You	6/24/78	8/19/78	1	28
Beast Of Burden	11/4/78	12/2/78	25	9
Ronstadt, Linda				
You're No Good	1/25/75	3/8/75	3	15
When Will I Be Loved	5/31/75	6/28/75	4	14
Heat Wave	10/18/75	11/15/75	5	15
That'll Be The Day	9/18/76	10/23/76	17	10
Someone To Lay Down Beside Me	1/29/77	2/5/77	38	3
Blue Bayou	11/5/77	12/17/77	7	17

Artist	Title	Debut	Peak	Pos	Wks
	It's So Easy	11/12/77	1/7/78	6	16
	Back In The U.S.A.	9/23/78	11/4/78	20	13
	Ooh Baby Baby	1/13/79	2/3/79	14	11

Rose Royce
	Car Wash	12/18/76	1/29/77	3	22
	I Wanna Get Next To You	4/16/77	5/21/77	22	10
	Do Your Dance—Part 1	11/12/77	11/26/77	38	3

Ross, Charlie
	Without Your Love (Mr. Jordan)	3/27/76	5/1/76	28	8

Ross, Diana
	Reach Out And Touch (Somebody's Hand)	4/27/70	6/1/70	15	9
	Ain't No Mountain High Enough	7/27/70	9/14/70	2	12
	Remember Me	12/28/70	2/1/71	4	10
	Reach Out I'll Be There	4/19/71	5/17/71	9	7
	Touch Me In The Morning	7/2/73	7/30/73	1	13
	Mahogany, Theme From (Do You Know Where You're Going To)	12/20/75	1/17/76	5	14
	Love Hangover	4/24/76	6/19/76	2	16
	The Boss	9/22/79	10/6/79	24	11

Ross, Diana & Marvin Gaye
	You're A Special Part Of Me	10/13/73	11/10/73	25	7

also see the Supremes

Roxy Music
	Love Is The Drug	2/14/76	4/3/76	32	10

Ruffin, David
	Walk Away From Love	12/27/75	1/24/76	10	11

also see the Temptations

Rufus
	Tell Me Something Good	8/10/74	8/31/74	2	12

Rufus featuring Chaka Khan
	You Got The Love	12/21/74	1/4/75	14	5
	Sweet Thing	2/14/76	4/3/76	14	14
	Stay	5/20/78	6/17/78	26	10

also see Khan, Chaka

Runt
	We Gotta Get You A Woman	1/11/71	2/8/71	11	7

Artist Title	Debut	Peak	Pos	Wks
Rundgren, Todd				
I Saw The Light	5/8/72	6/5/72	13	7
Hello, It's Me	10/20/73	12/15/73	1	16
Russell, Leon				
Tight Rope	10/2/72	10/16/72	8	6
Sailcat				
Motorcycle Mama	7/31/72	8/21/72	12	8
Sandpipers				
Come Saturday Morning	4/27/70	6/1/70	12	10
Sanford/Townsend Band				
Smoke From A Distant Fire	8/6/77	9/17/77	20	12
Sang, Samantha				
Emotion	1/14/78	4/15/78	1	26
Sans, Billie				
Solo	8/30/71	9/20/71	22	4
Santa Esmeralda				
Don't Let Me Be Misunderstood	12/24/77	1/28/78	20	12
Santana				
Evil Ways	2/16/70	3/16/70	14	8
Black Magic Woman	11/23/70	12/28/70	4	10
Oye Como Va	3/8/71	3/22/71	15	4
Everybody's Everything	10/18/71	11/22/71	8	8
She's Not There	12/17/77	1/7/78	37	5
Sayer, Leo				
Long Tall Glasses (I Can Dance)	4/26/75	6/7/75	2	15
You Make Me Feel Like Dancing	11/6/76	12/18/76	2	21
When I Need You	3/19/77	5/14/77	1	21
How Much Love	7/23/77	9/17/77	5	16
Thunder In My Heart	10/29/77	11/12/77	33	4
Scaggs, Boz				
Lowdown	8/28/76	10/2/76	7	14
Lido Shuffle	4/9/77	6/4/77	2	18
also see Miller, Steve				

Artist Title	Debut	Peak	Pos	Wks
Scott-Heron, Gil				
Angel Dust	11/18/78	12/2/78	33	10
Seals & Crofts				
Summer Breeze	11/6/72	12/4/72	5	8
Hummingbird	3/19/73	3/19/73	19	1
Diamond Girl	6/4/73	8/18/73	5	15
We May Never Pass The Way (Again)	9/22/73	11/17/73	8	13
Get Closer	6/19/76	8/21/76	2	18
Sebastian, John				
Welcome Back	4/17/76	5/8/76	1	14
Sedaka, Neil				
Laughter In The Rain	12/21/74	1/11/75	2	13
Bad Blood	10/4/75	10/25/75	1	20
Breaking Up Is Hard To Do	12/27/75	2/14/76	3	20
Love In The Shadows	5/8/76	6/26/76	8	12
Steppin' Out	6/26/76	7/10/76	35	5
You Gotta Make Your Own Sunshine	10/2/76	10/30/76	31	6
Amarillo	6/25/77	7/16/77	34	5
Seger, Bob				
Night Moves	1/15/77	3/12/77	3	19
Mainstreet	6/11/77	7/2/77	38	4
Still The Same	7/8/78	8/19/78	14	14
Hollywood Nights	9/23/78	10/21/78	22	12
We've Got Tonite	1/13/79	2/17/79	19	12
Shalamar				
Take That To The Bank	2/24/79	3/17/79	39	5
Shannon, Pat				
Back To Dreamin' Again	1/5/70	1/26/70	27	4
Sherman, Bobby				
La La La (If I Had You)	11/24/69	1/12/70	10	10
Easy Come, Easy Go	3/2/70	4/6/70	8	9
Hey, Mister Sun	5/25/70	6/22/70	14	8
Julie, Do Ya Love Me	8/24/70	9/21/70	3	9
Shocking Blue				
Venus	12/1/69	1/5/70	1	12

Artist	Title	Debut	Peak	Pos	Wks
Silver					
	Wham Bam	8/14/76	10/23/76	8	18
Silver Convention					
	Fly, Robin, Fly	11/22/75	12/13/75	8	15
	Get Up And Boogie (That's Right)	5/1/76	7/3/76	2	17
Simon, Carly					
	That's The Way I've Always Heard It Should Be	5/10/71	6/14/71	3	8
	Anticipation	1/24/72	2/21/72	6	9
	You're So Vain	12/11/72	1/8/73	1	14
	The Right Thing To Do	4/30/73	5/28/73	12	5
	Haven't Got Time For The Pain	6/8/74	6/22/74	21	5
	Nobody Does It Better	9/10/77	10/29/77	3	18
	You Belong To Me	6/17/78	8/5/78	11	17
Simon, Carly & James Taylor					
	Mockingbird	3/2/74	3/30/74	7	12
also see Taylor, James					
Simon, Joe					
	Drowning In The Sea Of Love	12/27/71	1/31/72	7	10
	Power Of Love	8/21/72	9/25/72	11	7
	Theme From Cleopatra Jones	9/22/73	10/13/73	26	4
Simon, Paul					
	Mother And Child Reunion	2/28/72	3/27/72	2	10
	Me And Julio Down By The Schoolyard	5/1/72	5/22/72	19	5
	Kodachrome	5/21/73	6/25/73	4	13
	Loves Me Like A Rock	8/18/73	9/29/73	1	13
	50 Ways To Leave Your Lover	1/10/76	2/7/76	1	20
	Slip Slidin' Away	12/24/77	2/4/78	13	11
also see Garfunkel, Art and Simon & Garfunkel					
Simon & Garfunkel					
	Bridge Over Troubled Water	1/26/70	2/16/70	1	13
	Cecilia	4/13/70	5/11/70	1	14
	El Condor Pasa	10/12/70	11/2/70	17	5
	My Little Town	12/6/75	1/10/76	5	15
also see Garfunkel, Art and Simon, Paul					

Artist	Title	Debut	Peak	Pos	Wks
Sister Sledge					
	He's The Greatest Dancer	4/21/79	5/26/79	17	15
	We Are Family	5/26/79	7/7/79	5	17
Skylark					
	Wildflower	4/16/73	5/28/73	6	9
Slave					
	Slide	8/6/77	8/20/77	36	5
Sly & the Family Stone					
	Thank You (Falettinme Be Mice Elf Agin)	1/5/70	1/26/70	1	12
	Family Affair	11/1/71	12/6/71	1	12
	Runnin' Away	3/6/72	3/20/72	24	4
	If You Want Me To Stay	6/18/73	6/25/73	22	9
Smith					
	Take A Look Around	2/16/70	3/16/70	19	6
Smith, Hurricane					
	Oh, Babe, What Would You Say	1/8/73	2/12/73	3	9
Smith, Rex					
	You Take My Breath Away	6/9/79	7/7/79	7	16
Smith, Sammi					
	Help Me Make It Through The Night	2/22/71	3/22/71	10	7
Sniff 'n' the Tears					
	Driver's Seat	9/22/79	10/20/79	21	9
Snow, Phoebe					
	Poetry Man	3/22/75	4/5/75	15	3
Sonny & Cher					
	All I Ever Need Is You	11/15/71	12/13/71	5	10
	A Cowboys Work Is Never Done	3/13/72	4/10/72	4	9
also see Cher					
Soul, David					
	Don't Give Up On Us	2/26/77	4/23/77	2	20
Sounds Of Sunshine					
	Love Means (You Never Have To Say You're Sorry)	7/12/71	7/12/71	27	2

Artist Title	Debut	Peak	Pos	Wks
South, Joe & the Believers				
Walk A Mile In My Shoes	12/22/69	1/26/70	12	9
Souther, J.D.				
You're Only Lonely	12/1/79	12/29/79	12	14
Sovine, Red				
Teddy Bear	7/10/76	8/7/76	15	10
Spinners				
I'll Be Around	10/16/72	11/20/72	2	8
Could It Be I'm Falling In Love	1/29/73	2/19/73	3	9
One Of A Kind (Love Affair)	6/4/73	6/11/73	9	7
They Just Can't Stop It The (Games People Play)	10/18/75	11/8/75	3	13
The Rubberband Man	11/6/76	12/25/76	4	18
also see Warwick, Dionne & Spinners				
Springfield, Rick				
Speak To The Sky	9/11/72	10/2/72	16	5
Stafford, Jim				
Spiders & Snakes	3/2/74	4/13/74	4	13
My Girl Bill	6/1/74	6/15/74	8	4
Stampeders				
Sweet City Woman	8/30/71	10/4/71	2	11
Staple Singers				
Respect Yourself	11/15/71	12/27/71	3	12
I'll Take You There	5/8/72	6/5/72	1	9
If You're Ready (Come Go With Me)	11/24/73	12/22/73	24	11
Let's Do It Again	11/22/75	12/20/75	7	11
Starbuck				
Moonlight Feels Right	6/19/76	7/31/76	21	12
Stargard				
Theme Song From "Which Way Is Up"	2/11/78	3/25/78	18	13
Starland Vocal Band				
Afternoon Delight	6/19/76	7/31/76	1	19

Artist	Title	Debut	Peak	Pos	Wks
Starr, Edwin					
	War	8/3/70	8/24/70	1	12
	Contact	3/10/79	3/24/79	29	7
Starr, Ringo					
	It Don't Come Easy	5/3/71	6/7/71	2	8
	Back Off Boogaloo	4/10/72	5/22/72	2	10
	Photograph	10/6/73	11/24/73	1	14
	You're Sixteen	12/15/73	2/9/74	2	16
	Oh My My	3/30/74	4/13/74	16	6
	No No Song	3/8/75	5/3/75	2	16
	A Dose Of Rock 'N' Roll	10/9/76	11/6/76	20	9
also see the Beatles					
Staton, Candi					
	Stand By Your Man	10/26/70	11/16/70	20	5
	Young Hearts Run Free	6/19/76	7/24/76	17	11
Stealers Wheel					
	Stuck In The Middle With You	4/9/73	5/21/73	4	8
also see Rafferty, Gerry					
Steam					
	Na Na Hey Hey Kiss Him Goodbye	10/27/69	12/1/69	1	13
Steely Dan					
	Do It Again	1/15/73	2/12/73	5	10
	Reeling In The Years	4/16/73	5/28/73	7	8
	Rikki Don't Lose That Number	6/29/74	7/13/74	3	11
	Peg	1/28/78	2/18/78	24	15
Steppenwolf					
	Hey Lawdy Mama	3/30/70	5/11/70	13	9
Stevens, Cat					
	Wild World	3/29/71	4/19/71	19	5
	Moon Shadow	7/5/71	8/2/71	13	6
	Peace Train	10/18/71	11/22/71	3	9
	Morning Has Broken	5/1/72	5/29/72	6	8
	Sitting	12/11/72	1/8/73	15	6
	The Hurt	8/25/73	9/22/73	11	9

Artist	Title	Debut	Peak	Pos	Wks
	Oh Very Young	6/8/74	6/8/74	19	1
	Another Saturday Night	9/28/74	11/2/74	4	13

Stevens, Ray
| | Everything Is Beautiful | 4/20/70 | 5/25/70 | 6 | 12 |
| | The Streak | 4/27/74 | 5/11/74 | 1 | 11 |

Henhouse Five Plus Too
| | In The Mood | 1/15/77 | 1/29/77 | 27 | 4 |

Stevenson, B.W.
| | My Maria | 9/15/73 | 10/13/73 | 13 | 8 |

Stewart, Al
| | Year Of The Cat | 1/29/77 | 3/12/77 | 2 | 17 |
| | Time Passages | 11/18/78 | 12/23/78 | 16 | 15 |

Stewart, Amii
| | Knock On Wood | 3/17/79 | 4/28/79 | 1 | 23 |

Stewart, John
| | Gold | 6/30/79 | 8/18/79 | 12 | 16 |

Stewart, Rod
	Maggie May	8/30/71	9/27/71	1	13
	/Reason To Believe	8/30/71	9/27/71	1	13
	You Wear It Well	9/18/72	10/16/72	11	7
	Tonight's The Night (Gonna Be Alright)	10/23/76	11/20/76	1	21
	The First Cut Is The Deepest	3/5/77	4/16/77	20	11
	You're In My Heart (The Final Acclaim)	11/26/77	1/28/78	3	21
	Hot Legs	4/8/78	5/6/78	23	8
	Da Ya Think I'm Sexy	1/20/79	2/24/79	1	23
	Ain't Love A Bitch	5/5/79	6/9/79	27	11

also see Faces

Stills, Stephen
| | Love The One You're With | 12/14/70 | 1/18/71 | 2 | 10 |
| | Marianne | 8/23/71 | 9/27/71 | 6 | 9 |

also see Crosby, Stills, Nash & Young

Stookey, Paul
| | Wedding Song (There Is Love) | 8/9/71 | 9/6/71 | 2 | 10 |

also see Peter, Paul & Mary

Artist	Title	Debut	Peak	Pos	Wks
Stories					
	Brother Louie	7/9/73	8/18/73	1	12
	Mammy Blue	11/10/73	12/22/73	15	11
Street People					
	Jennifer Tomkins	2/23/70	3/2/70	32	3
Streisand, Barbra					
	Stoney End	12/21/70	1/11/71	11	7
	The Way We Were	12/29/73	2/16/74	2	15
	Love Theme From "A Star Is Born" (Evergreen)	1/22/77	3/19/77	1	21
	My Heart Belongs To Me	7/2/77	8/27/77	18	13
	The Main Event/Fight	7/28/79	9/8/79	3	18
Barbra (Streisand) & Neil (Diamond)					
	You Don't Bring Me Flowers	11/11/78	12/23/78	1	20
Streisand, Barbra & Donna Summer					
	No More Tears (Enough Is Enough)	11/3/79	12/1/79	2	18
also see Diamond, Neil and Summer, Donna					
Strunk, Jud					
	Daisy A Day	4/23/73	4/30/73	18	2
Stylistics					
	You Are Everything	12/6/71	1/10/72	12	10
	Betcha By Golly, Wow	4/3/72	5/1/72	5	9
	People Make The World Go Round	7/17/72	7/24/72	21	2
	I'm Stone In Love With You	11/13/72	12/18/72	10	10
	Break Up To Make Up	3/12/73	4/2/73	8	6
	You'll Never Get To Heaven (If You Break My Heart)	6/25/73	7/2/73	27	2
	Rockin' Roll Baby	12/15/73	2/9/74	8	11
	You Make Me Feel Brand New	5/25/74	6/1/74	12	6
Styx					
	Lady	12/7/74	2/8/75	2	20
	Lorelei	3/20/76	4/17/76	8	14
	Mademoiselle	12/25/76	1/22/77	31	7
	Come Sail Away	10/15/77	12/10/77	3	26
	Blue Collar Man (Long Nights)	11/11/78	12/2/78	18	12
	Renegade	4/28/79	6/2/79	6	22
	Babe	10/6/79	11/24/79	1	26

Artist Title	Debut	Peak	Pos	Wks
Sugarhill Gang				
Rapper's Delight	11/10/79	12/22/79	17	18
Sugarloaf				
Green-Eyed Lady	9/28/70	10/19/70	2	11
Tongue In Cheek	2/15/71	2/15/71	31	1
Jerry Corbetta & Sugarloaf				
Don't Call Us, We'll Call You	3/29/75	4/26/75	5	12
Summer, Donna				
Love To Love You Baby	1/3/76	1/31/76	3	13
I Feel Love	10/1/77	11/12/77	4	16
Last Dance	6/10/78	7/22/78	4	33
MacArthur Park	10/14/78	12/9/78	2	23
Heaven Knows	2/10/79	3/24/79	8	19
Hot Stuff	5/5/79	6/16/79	1	24
Bad Girls	6/23/79	8/11/79	1	23
Dim All The Lights	9/29/79	11/24/79	12	18
also see Streisand, Barbra & Donna Summer				
Supertramp				
Give A Little Bit	7/30/77	8/20/77	25	8
The Logical Song	5/19/79	6/30/79	6	23
Goodbye Stranger	9/8/79	10/6/79	15	16
Take The Long Way Home	11/17/79	12/29/79	10	14
Supremes, Diana Ross & the				
Someday We'll Be Together	11/10/69	12/8/69	1	14
Supremes				
Up The Ladder To The Roof	3/9/70	4/20/70	3	12
Everybody's Got The Right To Love	7/27/70	7/27/70	31	2
Stoned Love	11/9/70	12/28/70	3	12
Nathan Jones	5/17/71	6/28/71	3	9
Floy Joy	2/21/72	3/13/72	14	6
Supremes & the Four Tops				
River Deep—Mountain High	11/30/70	12/28/70	11	8
also see the Four Tops and Ross, Diana				
Sutherland Brothers & Quiver				
(I Don't Want To Love You But) You Got Me Anyway	9/22/73	10/20/73	10	9

Artist	Title	Debut	Peak	Pos	Wks
Swan, Billy					
	I Can Help	11/30/74	12/21/74	4	14
Sweet					
	Little Willy	4/2/73	4/23/73	5	8
	Ballroom Blitz	9/13/75	10/18/75	2	21
	Fox On The Run	11/29/75	1/10/76	2	23
	Action	2/28/76	3/27/76	11	11
Sylvers					
	Boogie Fever	3/6/76	4/17/76	2	22
	Hot Line	12/4/76	2/12/77	1	26
	High School Dance	5/14/77	6/18/77	17	12
Sylvers, Foster					
	Misdemeanor	7/16/73	7/30/73	26	3
Sylvia					
	Pillow Talk	4/23/73	6/11/73	2	10
Taste Of Honey					
	Boogie Oogie Oogie	7/15/78	9/23/78	1	30
Tavares					
	It Only Takes A Minute	11/1/75	11/8/75	16	3
	Heaven Must Be Missing An Angel (Part 1)	7/31/76	9/11/76	20	12
	Never Had A Love	2/17/79	3/10/79	28	8
Taylor, James					
	Fire And Rain	9/28/70	11/2/70	2	10
	Country Road	2/15/71	3/8/71	15	5
	You've Got A Friend	6/14/71	7/5/71	2	9
	Don't Let Me Be Lonely Tonight	12/25/72	1/22/73	13	6
	How Sweet It Is (To Be Loved By You)	9/6/75	9/20/75	16	3
	Handy Man	7/23/77	9/10/77	3	16
	Your Smiling Face	11/26/77	12/24/77	24	9

also see Simon, Carly & James Taylor and Garfunkel, Art with James Taylor

Taylor, Johnnie					
	Jody's Got Your Girl And Gone	3/1/71	3/15/71	22	3
	I Believe In You (You Believe In Me)	7/16/73	9/1/73	10	10
	Disco Lady	2/28/76	4/17/76	4	18

Artist Title	Debut	Peak	Pos	Wks
Taylor, R. Dean				
Indiana Wants Me	9/7/70	10/4/70	4	9
Tchaikovsky, Bram				
Girl Of My Dreams	8/4/79	8/25/79	25	8
Tee Set				
Ma Belle Amie	1/12/70	2/16/70	9	11
Teegarden & Van Winkle				
God, Love And Rock & Roll	10/12/70	10/26/70	16	4
Temptations				
Psychedelic Shack	1/12/70	2/9/70	4	11
Ball Of Confusion (That's What The World Is Today)	5/25/70	7/13/70	3	13
Just My Imagination (Running Away With Me)	2/22/71	3/22/71	1	10
Superstar (Remember How You Got Where You Are)	11/22/71	12/13/71	13	6
Papa Was A Rollin' Stone	11/13/72	12/4/72	1	9
Masterpiece	3/19/73	4/30/73	9	7
also see Kendricks, Eddie and Ruffin, David				
10cc				
Rubber Bullets	9/29/73	11/3/73	23	9
I'm Not In Love	7/5/75	8/9/75	2	14
The Things We Do For Love	2/5/77	3/26/77	1	22
Ten Wheel Drive with Genya Ravan				
Morning Much Better	8/10/70	8/17/70	21	3
Tex, Joe				
I Gotcha	2/14/72	4/10/72	3	13
Thin Lizzy				
The Boys Are Back In Town	5/29/76	7/17/76	2	16
Thomas, B.J.				
Raindrops Keep Fallin' On My Head	11/17/69	12/22/69	2	13
Everybody's Out Of Town	4/6/70	4/27/70	32	4
I Just Can't Help Believing	7/20/70	8/24/70	2	12
Most Of All	12/28/70	1/25/71	18	6
No Love At All	3/29/71	4/12/71	14	5
Mighty Clouds Of Joy	7/19/71	8/2/71	9	5
Rock And Roll Lullaby	3/6/72	4/3/72	5	9

Artist	Title	Debut	Peak	Pos	Wks
	(Hey Won't You Play) Another Somebody Done Somebody Wrong Song	4/19/75	5/31/75	2	15
	Don't Worry Baby	8/27/77	10/15/77	19	12

Thomas, Ian
| | Painted Ladies | 11/10/73 | 12/15/73 | 11 | 13 |

Thomas, Rufus
| | Do The Funky Chicken | 2/16/70 | 3/9/70 | 28 | 4 |

Thomas, Timmy
| | Why Can't We Live Together | 12/25/72 | 1/29/73 | 5 | 10 |

Three Degrees
| | When Will I See You Again | 11/23/74 | 12/28/74 | 1 | 16 |

also see MFSB featuring the Three Degrees

Three Dog Night
	Celebrate	2/16/70	3/9/70	9	10
	Mama Told Me (Not To Come)	6/1/70	7/6/70	2	13
	Out In The Country	9/7/70	10/4/70	7	9
	One Man Band	11/30/70	12/14/70	15	5
	Joy To The World	3/22/71	4/19/71	1	13
	Liar	8/2/71	8/16/71	10	6
	An Old Fashioned Love Song	11/22/71	12/13/71	3	9
	Never Been To Spain	1/10/72	2/14/72	5	10
	The Family Of Man	3/27/72	5/1/72	6	10
	Black & White	8/28/72	9/18/72	1	8
	Pieces Of April	12/11/72	1/15/73	17	6
	Shambala	6/4/73	7/23/73	1	12
	Let Me Serenade You	10/27/73	12/8/73	11	12
	The Show Must Go On	5/4/74	5/25/74	6	9
	Sure As I'm Sittin' Here	8/17/74	8/17/74	17	1

Toby Beau
| | My Angel Baby | 8/12/78 | 9/9/78 | 20 | 11 |

Toto
| | Hold The Line | 12/23/78 | 2/3/79 | 6 | 19 |

Tower of Power
| | So Very Hard To Go | 6/18/73 | 7/9/73 | 17 | 6 |

Artist	Title	Debut	Peak	Pos	Wks
Trammps					
	Disco Inferno	6/3/78	7/8/78	23	12
Travolta, John					
	Let Her In	6/12/76	7/24/76	5	15
	All Strung Out On You	4/2/77	4/9/77	39	3
Travolta, John & Olivia Newton-John					
	You're The One That I Want	4/29/78	6/17/78	2	30
	Summer Nights	8/26/78	10/21/78	10	16
also see Newton-John, Olivia					
T. Rex					
	Hot Love	5/3/71	5/17/71	24	3
	Bang A Gong (Get It On)	2/21/72	3/13/72	4	7
True, Andrea, Connection					
	More, More, More Pt. 1	5/15/76	7/31/76	9	21
Turner, Ike & Tina					
	Proud Mary	2/8/71	3/1/71	6	7
Tyler, Bonnie					
	It's A Heartache	6/3/78	7/8/78	5	17
Undisputed Truth					
	Smiling Faces Sometimes	7/26/71	8/23/71	1	10
Valli, Frankie					
	My Eyes Adored You	2/15/75	3/22/75	2	15
	Swearin' To God	8/9/75	8/9/75	15	1
	Grease	7/8/78	8/12/78	3	21
also see the Four Seasons					
Van Halen					
	Dance The Night Away	6/23/79	7/28/79	14	14
Vanity Fare					
	Early In The Morning	11/17/69	12/15/69	16	9
	Hitchin' A Ride	3/30/70	6/1/70	1	16
Vannelli, Gino					
	I Just Wanna Stop	11/11/78	12/30/78	9	18
VanWarmer, Randy					
	Just When I Needed You Most	5/19/79	6/23/79	12	16

Artist	Title	Debut	Peak	Pos	Wks
Village People					
	Macho Man	9/2/78	10/21/78	3	38
	Y.M.C.A.	12/2/78	1/20/79	2	35
	In The Navy	4/7/79	5/12/79	10	19
Vinton, Bobby					
	My Elusive Dreams	1/19/70	2/9/70	15	7
	Every Day Of My Life	4/17/72	4/24/72	29	2
	Sealed With A Kiss	7/17/72	8/7/72	18	4
	My Melody Of Love	10/26/74	11/30/74	2	15
Wadsworth Mansion					
	Sweet Mary	1/25/71	2/22/71	5	8
Wakelin, Johnny & the Kinshasa Band					
	Black Superman—"Muhammad Ali"	8/30/75	9/27/75	9	6
Walker, Jr. & the All Stars					
	Gotta Hold On To This Feeling	2/23/70	3/16/70	17	6
	Take Me Girl, I'm Ready	8/2/71	9/13/71	7	9
Walsh, Joe					
	Rocky Mountain Way	10/6/73	11/3/73	24	7
	Life's Been Good	7/29/78	9/16/78	9	20
also see the Eagles					
War					
	All Day Music	8/9/71	9/13/71	4	9
	Slippin' Into Darkness	5/1/72	5/15/72	19	4
	The World Is A Ghetto	1/15/73	2/5/73	10	6
	The Cisco Kid	4/2/73	5/7/73	2	9
	Gypsy Man	7/23/73	9/1/73	11	11
	Me And Baby Brother	1/12/74	1/19/74	39	2
	Why Can't We Be Friends	7/19/75	8/16/75	6	14
	Summer	7/31/76	9/11/76	10	14
	Galaxy	3/4/78	3/18/78	37	5
also see Burdon, Eric & War					
Ward, Anita					
	Ring My Bell	6/9/79	7/21/79	1	18

Artist Title	Debut	Peak	Pos	Wks
Warnes, Jennifer				
Right Time Of The Night	3/19/77	5/28/77	8	18
I Know A Heartache When I See One	11/17/79	12/8/79	32	6
Warwick, Dionne				
I'll Never Fall In Love Again	12/22/69	2/2/70	6	10
I'll Never Love This Way Again	8/25/79	10/20/79	5	18
Deja Vu	12/29/79	2/2/80	15	13
Warwick, Dionne & Spinners				
Then Came You	8/31/74	10/12/74	6	13
also see the Spinners				
Wednesday				
Last Kiss	2/23/74	3/23/74	1	13
Weissberg, Eric & Steve Mandell				
Dueling Banjos	2/12/73	2/26/73	2	8
Welch, Bob				
Sentimental Lady	12/3/77	1/14/78	8	13
Ebony Eyes	3/25/78	5/6/78	10	14
also see Fleetwood Mac				
Welch, Lenny				
Breaking Up Is Hard To Do	1/19/70	2/16/70	31	5
Wet Willie				
Keep On Smilin'	8/31/74	8/31/74	15	1
Street Corner Serenade	2/18/78	2/25/78	42	2
White, Barry				
I'm Gonna Love You Just A Little More Baby	5/7/73	6/25/73	2	10
Never, Never Gonna Give Ya Up	12/8/73	2/16/74	10	13
Can't Get Enough Of Your Love, Babe	9/7/74	9/14/74	7	4
You're The First, The Last, My Everything	12/21/74	1/4/75	10	5
It's Ecstasy When You Lay Down Next To Me	9/17/77	10/29/77	17	12
also see the Love Unlimited Orchestra				
White Plains				
My Baby Loves Lovin'	5/4/70	6/22/70	2	11
also see the Brotherhood of Man, Edison Lighthouse, First Class and the Pipkins				

Artist	Title	Debut	Peak	Pos	Wks
Who					
	The Seeker	5/4/70	5/11/70	33	3
	Summertime Blues	7/20/70	8/3/70	16	6
	See Me, Feel Me	11/2/70	11/30/70	5	8
	Won't Get Fooled Again	7/26/71	8/16/71	15	5
	Join Together	8/21/72	9/4/72	21	3
	Squeeze Box	1/10/76	3/13/76	17	16
	Who Are You	10/7/78	11/11/78	13	15
Wild Cherry					
	Play That Funky Music	8/7/76	9/25/76	2	27
Williams, Andy					
	(Where Do I Begin) Love Story	3/1/71	4/5/71	12	7
Williams, Deniece					
	Free	2/12/77	3/19/77	27	9
	Baby, Baby My Love's For Real	3/4/78	3/18/78	41	3
	also see Mathis, Johnny & Deniece Williams				
Williams, John					
	Star Wars (Main Title)	8/6/77	9/17/77	11	20
	Theme From "Close Encounters Of The Third Kind"	1/14/78	3/4/78	10	16
Wilson, Al					
	Show And Tell	11/17/73	12/29/73	2	14
Wilson, Meri					
	Telephone Man	8/20/77	9/3/77	35	4
Wilton Place Street Band					
	Disco Lucy (I Love Lucy Theme)	3/26/77	4/16/77	40	4
Wing And A Prayer Fife & Drum Corps					
	Baby Face	3/13/76	4/24/76	17	12
Winter, Edgar, Group					
	Frankenstein	4/16/73	5/28/73	1	11
	Free Ride	9/15/73	10/27/73	4	13
Withers, Bill					
	Ain't No Sunshine	7/26/71	9/13/71	2	12
	Lean On Me	5/29/72	7/17/72	1	13
	Use Me	9/18/72	10/23/72	2	8

Artist	Title	Debut	Peak	Pos	Wks
	Kissing My Love	3/5/73	3/12/73	20	3
	Lovely Day	1/28/78	2/25/78	29	9

Womack, Bobby

| | Lookin' For A Love | 4/6/74 | 5/4/74 | 13 | 6 |

Wonder, Stevie

	Yester-Me, Yester-You, Yesterday	11/3/69	12/15/69	4	11
	Never Had A Dream Come True	2/2/70	3/9/70	23	6
	Signed, Sealed, Delivered I'm Yours	6/29/70	8/17/70	2	13
	Heaven Help Us All	10/26/70	11/16/70	6	8
	We Can Work It Out	3/15/71	4/5/71	10	5
	If You Really Love Me	9/20/71	10/18/71	4	9
	Superstition	12/11/72	1/29/73	1	12
	You Are The Sunshine Of My Life	4/2/73	5/21/73	1	9
	Higher Ground	9/1/73	9/29/73	9	11
	Living For The City	12/1/73	1/12/74	13	12
	Don't You Worry 'Bout A Thing	6/1/74	6/15/74	11	3
	You Haven't Done Nothin	10/5/74	10/5/74	14	1
	Boogie On Reggae Woman	2/8/75	2/8/75	15	2
	I Wish	12/11/76	2/12/77	5	17
	Sir Duke	4/9/77	6/4/77	1	18
	Send One Your Love	12/1/79	1/19/80	20	13

Wright, Betty

| | Clean Up Woman | 12/27/71 | 1/31/72 | 6 | 11 |
| | Tonight's The Night | 10/21/78 | 11/18/78 | 29 | 7 |

also see Brown, Peter with Betty Wright

Wright, Charles, & the Watts 103rd Street Rhythm Band

| | Love Land | 6/8/70 | 7/6/70 | 13 | 8 |

Wright, Gary

| | Dream Weaver | 2/14/76 | 3/27/76 | 4 | 17 |
| | Love Is Alive | 5/22/76 | 7/17/76 | 12 | 17 |

Yes

| | Roundabout | 3/13/72 | 4/10/72 | 7 | 9 |

Young, John Paul

| | Love Is In The Air | 10/14/78 | 11/18/78 | 15 | 14 |

Artist	Title	Debut	Peak	Pos	Wks
Young, Neil					
	Heart Of Gold	2/21/72	3/13/72	1	11
also see Crosby, Stills, Nash & Young					
Zevon, Warren					
	Werewolves Of London	6/3/78	6/17/78	32	8
ZZ Top					
	La Grange	6/15/74	6/29/74	4	10
	Tush	8/30/75	9/13/75	5	12
	It's Only Love	10/23/76	11/13/76	31	5

ALPHABETICAL LISTING BY TITLE

Debut	Peak	Title	Artist	Pos	Wks
3/9/70	4/13/70	ABC	Jackson 5	1	12
12/29/73	2/16/74	Abra-Ca-Dabra	DeFranco Family featuring Tony DeFranco	5	14
10/4/71	11/15/71	Absolutely Right	Five Man Electrical Band	5	10
2/28/76	3/27/76	Action	Sweet	11	11
3/9/70	3/9/70	Add Some Music To Your Day	Beach Boys	39	2
11/9/70	12/14/70	After Midnight	Eric Clapton	4	10
8/11/79	9/15/79	After The Love Has Gone	Earth, Wind & Fire	12	18
12/18/76	3/5/77	After The Lovin'	Engelbert Humperdinck	6	24
6/19/76	7/31/76	Afternoon Delight	Starland Vocal Band	1	19
3/4/78	3/25/78	Ain't Gonna' Hurt Nobody	Brick	29	9
5/5/79	6/9/79	Ain't Love A Bitch	Rod Stewart	27	11
7/27/70	9/14/70	Ain't No Mountain High Enough	Diana Ross	2	12
6/9/79	7/7/79	Ain't No Stoppin' Us Now	McFadden & Whitehead	20	14
7/26/71	9/13/71	Ain't No Sunshine	Bill Withers	2	12
10/11/75	10/25/75	Ain't No Way To Treat A Lady	Helen Reddy	11	5
3/5/73	4/9/73	Ain't No Woman (Like The One I've Got)	Four Tops	2	10
1/31/72	2/28/72	Ain't Understanding Mellow	Jerry Butler & Brenda Lee Eager	17	6
7/13/74	8/24/74	Air That I Breathe, The	Hollies	2	13
4/6/70	5/18/70	Airport Love Theme	Vincent Bell	16	11
6/14/71	6/14/71	Albert Flasher	Guess Who	31	1
11/25/78	12/23/78	Alive Again	Chicago	17	11
12/27/75	3/20/76	All By Myself	Eric Carmen	4	22
8/9/71	9/13/71	All Day Music	War	4	9
11/15/71	12/13/71	All I Ever Need Is You	Sonny & Cher	5	10
2/2/70	3/16/70	All I Have To Do Is Dream	Bobbie Gentry & Glen Campbell	11	9
9/29/73	11/10/73	All I Know	Art Garfunkel	6	12

Debut	Peak	Title	Artist	Pos	Wks
10/13/79	10/20/79	All Of My Love	Led Zeppelin	47	2
9/14/70	10/4/70	All Right Now	Free	2	10
4/2/77	4/9/77	All Strung Out On You	John Travolta	39	3
7/3/72	7/31/72	Alone Again (Naturally)	Gilbert O'Sullivan	1	13
2/19/73	4/2/73	Also Sprach Zarathustra (2001)	Deodato	1	9
1/28/78	3/11/78	Always And Forever	Heatwave	19	23
1/19/70	2/9/70	Always Something There To Remind Me	R.B. Greaves	19	6
6/25/77	7/16/77	Amarillo	Neil Sedaka	34	5
11/6/72	11/6/72	American City Suite	Cashman & West	21	1
12/6/71	1/3/72	American Pie—Parts I & II	Don McLean	1	16
3/16/70	5/4/70	American Woman	Guess Who	1	14
1/5/74	2/2/74	Americans	Byron MacGregor	5	8
1/25/71	3/1/71	Amos Moses	Jerry Reed	2	10
6/4/73	6/4/73	And I Love You So	Perry Como	28	3
9/1/73	9/8/73	Angel	Aretha Franklin	28	4
11/18/78	12/2/78	Angel Dust	Gil Scott-Heron	33	10
4/23/77	7/30/77	Angel In Your Arms	Hot	7	23
9/22/73	10/27/73	Angie	Rolling Stones	2	12
11/16/74	12/14/74	Angie Baby	Helen Reddy	4	15
8/30/71	9/13/71	Annabella	Hamilton, Joe Frank & Reynolds	23	3
7/29/78	8/12/78	Annie Mae	Natalie Cole	32	7
7/6/74	7/20/74	Annie's Song	John Denver	2	11
3/15/71	4/5/71	Another Day	Paul McCartney	3	7
6/15/74	6/15/74	Another Park, Another Sunday	Doobie Brothers	17	1
9/28/74	11/2/74	Another Saturday Night	Cat Stevens	4	13
1/24/72	2/21/72	Anticipation	Carly Simon	6	9
8/11/79	9/1/79	Anybody Wanna Party	Gloria Gaynor	34	9
4/19/75	5/31/75	Another Somebody Done Somebody Wrong Song	B.J. Thomas	2	15
1/20/79	2/24/79	Aqua Boogie	Parliament	21	12
1/5/74	1/19/74	Are You Lonesome Tonight	Donny Osmond	35	3
8/18/73	9/1/73	Are You Man Enough	Four Tops	15	7
6/22/70	7/27/70	Are You Ready	Pacific Gas & Electric	15	9
6/11/77	8/20/77	Ariel	Dean Friedman	4	19
1/19/70	2/16/70	Arizona	Mark Lindsay	7	9
4/30/73	4/30/73	Armed And Extremely Dangerous	First Choice	25	2
5/15/72	6/12/72	Ask Me What You Want	Millie Jackson	16	6
9/6/75	9/27/75	At Seventeen	Janis Ian	4	12
2/26/73	3/19/73	Aubrey	Bread	16	6
5/3/75	5/17/75	Autobahn	Kraftwerk	12	4
10/6/79	11/24/79	Babe	Styx	1	26
3/4/78	3/18/78	Baby, Baby My Love's For Real	Deniece Williams	41	3
4/3/72	5/1/72	Baby Blue	Badfinger	2	10

Debut	Peak	Title	Artist	Pos	Wks
11/13/76	12/18/76	Baby Boy	Mary Kay Place	24	8
12/3/77	2/4/78	Baby Come Back	Player	4	24
8/14/72	9/25/72	Baby Don't Get Hooked On Me	Mac Davis	1	12
3/13/76	4/24/76	Baby Face	Wing And A Prayer Fife & Drum Corps	17	12
8/7/76	9/18/76	Baby, I Love Your Way	Peter Frampton	6	14
10/25/71	11/29/71	Baby I'm-A Want You	Bread	2	11
7/31/72	8/28/72	Baby Let Me Take You (In My Arms)	Detroit Emeralds	18	6
2/2/70	2/23/70	Baby Take Me In Your Arms	Jefferson	29	4
10/22/77	11/26/77	Baby, What A Big Surprise	Chicago	12	12
11/9/74	11/23/74	Back Home Again	John Denver	9	4
11/12/77	12/24/77	Back In Love Again	L.T.D.	22	13
9/23/78	11/4/78	Back In The U.S.A.	Linda Ronstadt	20	13
4/10/72	5/22/72	Back Off Boogaloo	Ringo Starr	2	10
8/14/72	9/18/72	Back Stabbers	O'Jays	2	10
1/5/70	1/26/70	Back To Dreamin' Again	Pat Shannon	27	4
5/28/77	6/18/77	Back Together Again	Daryl Hall & John Oates	32	5
6/4/73	7/2/73	Back When My Hair Was Short	Gunhill Road	17	5
6/4/73	7/16/73	Bad, Bad Leroy Brown	Jim Croce	1	12
10/4/75	10/25/75	Bad Blood	Neil Sedaka	1	20
9/22/79	10/20/79	Bad Case Of Loving You (Doctor, Doctor)	Robert Palmer	11	15
6/23/79	8/11/79	Bad Girls	Donna Summer	1	23
5/3/75	6/21/75	Bad Time	Grand Funk	4	15
6/10/78	7/8/78	Baker Street	Gerry Rafferty	4	22
5/25/70	7/13/70	Ball Of Confusion	Temptations	3	13
9/13/75	10/18/75	Ballroom Blitz	Sweet	2	21
6/1/70	7/20/70	Band Of Gold	Freda Payne	2	14
5/11/74	6/15/74	Band On The Run	Paul McCartney & Wings	1	15
2/21/72	3/13/72	Bang A Gong (Get It On)	T. Rex	4	7
12/8/69	1/12/70	Barbara, I Love You	New Colony Six	13	8
5/15/76	6/26/76	Baretta's Theme	Rhythm Heritage	21	9
6/18/77	7/30/77	Barracuda	Heart	6	16
9/22/73	11/3/73	Basketball Jones	Cheech & Chong	2	12
10/20/73	12/1/73	Be	Neil Diamond	8	10
11/16/70	12/14/70	Be My Baby	Andy Kim	7	8
6/22/74	6/22/74	Be Thankful For What You Got	William DeVaughn	22	3
9/7/74	10/26/74	Beach Baby	First Class	1	15
11/4/78	12/2/78	Beast Of Burden	Rolling Stones	25	9
8/7/72	9/25/72	Beautiful Sunday	Daniel Boone	10	11
6/7/75	6/7/75	Before The Next Teardrop Falls	Freddy Fender	13	1
6/21/71	8/2/71	Beginnings	Chicago	3	11
7/9/73	7/30/73	Behind Closed Doors	Charlie Rich	22	3
7/16/73	9/1/73	Believe In Humanity	Carole King	25	7
3/23/70	4/13/70	Bells, The	Originals	23	6
9/18/72	10/16/72	Ben	Michael Jackson	1	9

Debut	Peak	Title	Artist	Pos	Wks
3/9/74	4/6/74	Bennie And The Jets	Elton John	1	15
1/11/75	2/8/75	Best Of My Love	Eagles	3	15
7/16/77	9/17/77	Best Of My Love	Emotions	1	19
4/13/74	5/11/74	Best Thing That Ever Happened To Me	Gladys Knight & the Pips	8	10
4/3/72	5/1/72	Betcha By Golly, Wow	Stylistics	5	9
9/25/76	12/11/76	Beth	Kiss	3	24
12/16/78	1/20/79	Bicycle Race	Queen	20	11
2/19/73	3/19/73	Big City Miss Ruth Ann	Gallery	15	5
3/17/79	4/14/79	Big Shot	Billy Joel	19	11
7/20/70	8/17/70	Big Yellow Taxi	Neighborhood	11	7
5/18/74	6/8/74	Billy, Don't Be A Hero	Bo Donaldson & the Heywoods	1	14
9/27/71	10/18/71	Birds Of A Feather	Raiders	15	7
9/21/74	11/2/74	Bitch Is Back, The	Elton John	1	16
2/19/77	3/12/77	Bite Your Lip (Get Up And Dance!)	Elton John	28	5
8/28/72	9/18/72	Black & White	Three Dog Night	1	8
7/9/77	9/24/77	Black Betty	Ram Jam	2	20
12/27/71	1/31/72	Black Dog	Led Zeppelin	4	10
11/23/70	12/28/70	Black Magic Woman	Santana	4	10
8/30/75	9/27/75	Black Superman— "Muhammad Ali"	Johnny Wakelin & the Kinshasa Band	9	6
2/1/75	2/22/75	Black Water	Doobie Brothers	1	18
12/4/76	1/1/77	Blinded By The Light	Manfred Mann's Earth Band	1	20
4/14/79	5/26/79	Blow Away	George Harrison	16	17
1/5/70	2/2/70	Blowing Away	Fifth Dimension	9	7
11/5/77	12/17/77	Blue Bayou	Linda Ronstadt	7	17
11/11/78	12/2/78	Blue Collar Man (Long Nights)	Styx	18	12
2/15/71	3/15/71	Blue Money	Van Morrison	7	8
4/30/73	5/7/73	Blue Suede Shoes	Johnny Rivers	23	2
7/15/78	8/19/78	Bluer Than Blue	Michael Johnson	19	11
2/21/76	4/3/76	Bohemian Rhapsody	Queen	1	22
2/12/77	3/12/77	Boogie Child	Bee Gees	23	7
2/2/74	3/2/74	Boogie Down	Eddie Kendricks	7	8
3/6/76	4/17/76	Boogie Fever	Sylvers	2	22
9/24/77	11/26/77	Boogie Nights	Heatwave	1	23
2/8/75	2/8/75	Boogie On Reggae Woman	Stevie Wonder	15	2
7/15/78	9/23/78	Boogie Oogie Oogie	Taste Of Honey	1	30
6/16/79	7/14/79	Boogie Wonderland	Earth, Wind & Fire with the Emotions	12	18
6/11/73	7/16/73	Boogie Woogie Bugle Boy	Bette Midler	2	10
3/11/78	4/22/78	Bootzilla	Bootsy's Rubber Band	24	12
12/28/70	2/8/71	Born To Wander	Rare Earth	2	11
9/22/79	10/6/79	Boss, The	Diana Ross	24	11
5/29/76	7/17/76	Boys Are Back In Town, The	Thin Lizzy	2	16
7/6/70	7/27/70	Boys In The Band, The	Boys In The Band	26	4
11/22/71	12/20/71	Brand New Key	Melanie	1	12

Debut	Peak	Title	Artist	Pos	Wks
7/3/72	8/28/72	Brandy (You're A Fine Girl)	Looking Glass	1	14
3/12/73	4/2/73	Break Up To Make Up	Stylistics	8	6
7/31/72	8/7/72	Breaking Up Is Hard To Do	Partridge Family	22	2
12/27/75	2/14/76	Breaking Up Is Hard To Do	Neil Sedaka	3	20
1/19/70	2/16/70	Breaking Up Is Hard To Do	Lenny Welch	31	5
10/1/77	11/12/77	Brick House	Commodores	21	11
4/26/71	5/24/71	Bridge Over Troubled Water	Aretha Franklin	11	6
1/26/70	2/16/70	Bridge Over Troubled Water	Simon & Garfunkel	1	13
6/7/71	7/5/71	Bring The Boys Home	Freda Payne	17	6
11/17/79	12/15/79	Broken Hearted Me	Anne Murray	24	10
7/9/73	8/18/73	Brother Louie	Stories	1	12
6/19/72	6/26/72	Brown Eyed Girl	El Chicano	25	2
4/19/71	5/31/71	Brown Sugar	Rolling Stones	1	11
12/28/74	2/8/75	Bungle In The Jungle	Jethro Tull	7	13
8/14/72	10/30/72	Burning Love	Elvis Presley	2	14
3/10/79	3/24/79	Bustin' Loose Part 1	Chuck Brown & the Soul Searchers	27	10
3/2/70	4/6/70	Call Me	Aretha Franklin	28	7
3/12/73	4/2/73	Call Me (Come Back Home)	Al Green	10	6
8/17/74	8/24/74	Call On Me	Chicago	23	3
4/9/77	5/21/77	Calling Dr. Love	Kiss	5	16
8/24/70	9/28/70	Candida	Dawn	1	12
5/8/72	6/26/72	Candy Man, The	Sammy Davis Jr.	2	11
10/5/74	11/2/74	Can't Get Enough	Bad Company	6	12
9/7/74	9/14/74	Can't Get Enough Of Your Love, Babe	Barry White	7	4
3/1/75	3/29/75	Can't Get It Out Of My Head	Electric Light Orchestra	14	5
2/18/78	4/15/78	Can't Smile Without You	Barry Manilow	4	25
4/2/77	5/7/77	Can't Stop Dancin'	Captain & Tennille	7	14
11/30/70	12/14/70	Can't Stop Loving You	Tom Jones	20	4
12/18/76	1/29/77	Car Wash	Rose Royce	3	22
1/22/77	3/19/77	Carry On Wayward Son	Kansas	2	20
4/3/72	5/8/72	Castles In The Air	Don McLean	14	8
9/3/77	10/8/77	Cat Scratch Fever	Ted Nugent	31	8
11/16/74	12/21/74	Cat's In The Cradle	Harry Chapin	1	16
4/13/70	5/11/70	Cecilia	Simon & Garfunkel	1	14
2/16/70	3/9/70	Celebrate	Three Dog Night	9	10
10/4/71	10/25/71	Charity Ball	Fanny	3	9
6/22/70	7/13/70	Check Out Your Mind	Impressions	23	4
10/25/71	12/20/71	Cherish	David Cassidy	3	15
4/23/73	5/7/73	"Cherry Cherry" from Hot August Night	Neil Diamond	20	5
4/5/75	5/10/75	Chevy Van	Sammy Johns	5	14

Debut	Peak	Title	Artist	Pos	Wks
4/5/71	5/3/71	Chick-A-Boom	Daddy Dewdrop	5	8
9/8/73	10/13/73	China Grove	Doobie Brothers	5	12
9/6/71	9/27/71	Chirpy Chirpy Cheep Cheep	Mac & Katie Kissoon	12	6
7/30/77	8/20/77	Christine Sixteen	Kiss	26	8
6/9/79	7/21/79	Chuck E.'s In Love	Rickie Lee Jones	10	16
4/30/77	5/14/77	Cinderella	Firefall	32	7
4/2/73	5/7/73	Cisco Kid, The	War	2	9
9/25/72	10/2/72	City Of New Orleans, The	Arlo Guthrie	22	5
11/13/72	12/25/72	Clair	Gilbert O'Sullivan	2	13
10/5/74	10/26/74	Clap For The Wolfman	Guess Who	12	7
12/27/71	1/31/72	Clean Up Woman	Betty Wright	6	11
9/22/73	10/13/73	Cleopatra Jones, Theme From	Joe Simon	26	4
1/14/78	3/4/78	Close Encounters Of The Third Kind, Theme From	John Williams	10	16
7/1/78	7/29/78	Close The Door	Teddy Pendergrass	19	15
6/29/70	7/20/70	(They Long To Be) Close To You	Carpenters	1	13
3/18/78	5/20/78	Closer I Get To You, The	Roberta Flack & Donny Hathaway	6	21
9/7/70	9/7/70	Closer To Home	Grand Funk Railroad	31	1
7/24/72	8/28/72	Coconut	Nilsson	9	7
8/20/77	10/22/77	Cold As Ice	Foreigner	6	17
8/9/71	8/9/71	Colour My World	Chicago	7	4
2/23/70	4/6/70	Come And Get It	Badfinger	3	11
3/30/74	5/4/74	Come And Get Your Love	Redbone	2	13
6/18/77	7/16/77	Come In From The Rain	Captain & Tennille	24	8
5/1/76	5/22/76	Come On Over	Olivia Newton-John	25	7
4/13/70	4/20/70	Come Running	Van Morrison	36	2
10/15/77	12/10/77	Come Sail Away	Styx	3	26
4/27/70	6/1/70	Come Saturday Morning	Sandpipers	12	10
11/10/79	12/1/79	Come To Me	France Joli	18	11
10/6/69	11/3/69	Come Together	Beatles	1	16
7/3/72	7/31/72	Conquistador	Procol Harum	12	6
3/10/79	3/24/79	Contact	Edwin Starr	29	7
12/13/75	12/27/75	Convoy	C.W. McCall	1	22
12/22/79	1/26/80	Cool Change	Little River Band	24	11
7/1/78	7/29/78	Copacabana (At The Copa)	Barry Manilow	9	19
12/4/72	12/11/72	Corner Of The Sky	Jackson 5	16	4
1/29/73	2/19/73	Could It Be I'm Falling In Love	Spinners	3	9
8/9/75	9/13/75	Could It Be Magic	Barry Manilow	6	14
4/2/77	6/11/77	Couldn't Get It Right	Climax Blues Band	4	17
5/13/78	6/10/78	Count On Me	Jefferson Starship	21	12
12/20/75	1/3/76	Country Boy (You Got Your Feet In L.A.)	Glen Campbell	12	10
2/15/71	3/8/71	Country Road	James Taylor	15	5
6/12/72	6/26/72	Country Woman	Magic Lanterns	22	3
12/15/79	1/26/80	Coward Of The County	Kenny Rogers	2	22

Debut	Peak	Title	Artist	Pos	Wks
3/13/72	4/10/72	Cowboys Work Is Never Done, A	Sonny & Cher	4	9
2/5/77	3/12/77	Crackerbox Palace	George Harrison	15	12
8/31/70	10/4/70	Cracklin' Rosie	Neil Diamond	1	11
8/2/71	8/2/71	Crazy About The La La La	Smokey Robinson & the Miracles	32	1
11/6/72	12/4/72	Crazy Horses	Osmonds	18	5
3/24/79	4/14/79	Crazy Love	Poco	17	13
3/20/72	4/3/72	Crazy Mama	J.J. Cale	12	4
6/12/76	8/7/76	Crazy On You	Heart	3	18
1/8/73	2/5/73	Crocodile Rock	Elton John	1	12
9/22/79	10/20/79	Cruel To Be Kind	Nick Lowe	15	12
11/22/71	12/13/71	Crunchy Granola Suite	Neil Diamond	9	8
11/2/70	11/23/70	Cry Me A River	Joe Cocker	7	6
12/22/69	12/29/69	Cupid	Johnny Nash	35	3
5/28/77	6/18/77	Da Doo Ron Ron	Shaun Cassidy	1	23
1/20/79	2/24/79	Da Ya Think I'm Sexy	Rod Stewart	1	23
6/11/73	6/18/73	Daddy Could Swear, I Declare	Gladys Knight & the Pips	23	5
6/19/72	8/7/72	Daddy Don't You Walk So Fast	Wayne Newton	3	11
1/29/73	3/19/73	Daddy's Home	Jermaine Jackson	8	9
4/23/73	4/30/73	Daisy A Day	Jud Strunk	18	2
1/21/78	3/18/78	Dance, Dance, Dance	Chic	7	24
6/23/79	7/28/79	Dance The Night Away	Van Halen	14	14
3/11/78	7/1/78	Dance With Me	Peter Brown with Betty Wright	11	28
9/27/75	10/25/75	Dance With Me	Orleans	2	13
1/4/75	2/1/75	Dancin' Fool	Guess Who	14	5
4/30/77	5/28/77	Dancin' Man	Q	29	7
3/31/79	3/31/79	Dancin' Shoes	Nigel Olsson	44	1
1/8/73	2/5/73	Dancing In The Moonlight	King Harvest	12	10
5/4/74	6/15/74	Dancing Machine	Jackson 5	4	13
2/5/77	4/9/77	Dancing Queen	ABBA	1	20
4/30/73	6/11/73	Daniel	Elton John	3	9
2/26/73	4/16/73	Danny's Song	Anne Murray	5	10
1/19/74	3/2/74	Dark Lady	Cher	3	13
4/20/70	6/8/70	Daughter 0f Darkness	Tom Jones	2	12
12/13/71	1/17/72	Day After Day	Badfinger	2	14
6/26/72	8/7/72	Day By Day	Godspell	10	9
3/20/72	5/8/72	Day Dreaming	Aretha Franklin	2	12
3/27/72	4/17/72	Day I Found Myself, The	Honey Cone	21	5
10/15/77	11/19/77	Daybreak	Barry Manilow	8	15
12/18/76	1/22/77	Dazz	Brick	3	14
1/10/76	2/28/76	December, 1963 (Oh, What A Night)	Four Seasons	1	24
3/12/77	3/26/77	Dedication	Bay City Rollers	38	4
8/16/71	9/13/71	Deep Blue	George Harrison	15	6
3/13/76	4/24/76	Deep Purple	Donny & Marie Osmond	7	16
9/21/70	11/2/70	Deeper & Deeper	Freda Payne	7	11
5/5/79	6/23/79	Deeper Than The Night	Olivia Newton-John	29	12

Debut	Peak	Title	Artist	Pos	Wks
12/29/79	2/2/80	Deja Vu	Dionne Warwick	15	13
7/23/73	9/15/73	Delta Dawn	Helen Reddy	3	12
12/31/77	2/11/78	Desiree	Neil Diamond	22	13
8/11/79	9/22/79	Devil Went Down To Georgia, The	Charlie Daniels Band	2	23
8/21/76	10/9/76	Devil Woman	Cliff Richard	2	19
11/27/72	12/11/72	Dialogue (Part I & II)	Chicago	17	4
6/4/73	8/18/73	Diamond Girl	Seals & Crofts	5	15
5/15/72	6/5/72	Diary	Bread	15	6
10/9/76	10/30/76	Did You Boogie (With Your Baby)	Flash Cadillac & the Continental Kids	33	6
2/2/70	3/2/70	Didn't I (Blow Your Mind This Time)	Delfonics	7	10
9/29/79	11/24/79	Dim All The Lights	Donna Summer	12	18
10/20/79	11/17/79	Dirty White Boy	Foreigner	25	9
9/11/76	10/9/76	Disco Duck (Part 1)	Rick Dees & his Cast of Idiots	1	24
6/3/78	7/8/78	Disco Inferno	Trammps	23	12
2/28/76	4/17/76	Disco Lady	Johnnie Taylor	4	18
3/26/77	4/16/77	Disco Lucy (I Love Lucy Theme)	Wilton Place Street Band	40	4
3/24/79	5/26/79	Disco Nights (Rock-Freak)	GQ	14	21
11/30/74	12/21/74	Do It ('Til You're Satisfied)	B.T. Express	8	6
1/15/73	2/12/73	Do It Again	Steely Dan	5	10
7/7/79	8/4/79	Do It Or Die	Atlanta Rhythm Section	19	11
12/8/79	2/16/80	Do That To Me One More Time	Captain & Tennille	5	21
2/16/70	3/9/70	Do The Funky Chicken	Rufus Thomas	28	4
9/14/70	10/4/70	Do What You Wanna Do	Five Flights Up	6	7
3/5/77	4/16/77	Do Ya	Electric Light Orchestra	24	10
8/27/77	10/22/77	Do Ya Wanna Get Funky With Me	Peter Brown	3	18
4/15/78	5/6/78	Do You Believe In Magic	Shaun Cassidy	22	11
10/9/76	11/20/76	Do You Feel Like We Do	Peter Frampton	9	14
9/6/71	10/11/71	Do You Know What I Mean	Lee Michaels	2	11
5/24/71	6/21/71	Do You Know What Time It Is	P-Nut Gallery	8	6
9/8/79	10/6/79	Do You Think I'm Disco	Steve Dahl & Teenage Radiation	5	19
6/4/77	8/6/77	Do You Wanna Make Love	Peter McCann	4	20
2/5/73	3/12/73	Do You Want To Dance	Bette Midler	12	6
11/12/77	11/26/77	Do Your Dance—Part 1	Rose Royce	38	3
4/3/72	4/24/72	Doctor My Eyes	Jackson Browne	4	9
1/18/75	2/22/75	Doctor's Orders	Carol Douglas	7	11
11/23/70	12/14/70	Does Anybody Really Know What Time It Is	Chicago	3	8
7/21/79	8/18/79	Does Your Mother Know	ABBA	28	11
2/1/71	3/8/71	Doesn't Somebody Want To Be Wanted	Partridge Family	1	11
11/23/70	1/4/71	Domino	Van Morrison	3	11
5/10/71	5/10/71	Done Too Soon	Neil Diamond	32	1

Debut	Peak	Title	Artist	Pos	Wks
8/4/79	10/13/79	Don't Bring Me Down	Electric Light Orchestra	5	24
3/29/75	4/26/75	Don't Call Us, We'll Call You	Sugarloaf/Jerry Corbetta	5	12
11/24/69	1/12/70	Don't Cry Daddy	Elvis Presley	4	11
3/3/79	3/31/79	Don't Cry Out Loud	Melissa Manchester	13	14
12/22/79	2/9/80	Don't Do Me Like That	Tom Petty & the Heartbreakers	6	21
10/9/72	10/30/72	Don't Ever Be Lonely (A Poor Little Fool Like Me)	Cornelius Brothers & Sister Rose	21	4
1/22/73	2/19/73	Don't Expect Me To Be Your Friend	Lobo	4	8
2/26/77	4/23/77	Don't Give Up On Us	David Soul	2	20
7/24/76	8/14/76	Don't Go Breaking My Heart	Elton John & Kiki Dee	1	20
10/8/77	12/10/77	Don't It Make My Brown Eyes Blue	Crystal Gayle	1	21
5/17/71	6/21/71	Don't Knock My Love	Wilson Pickett	7	8
3/5/77	4/16/77	Don't Leave Me This Way	Thelma Houston	4	17
12/1/79	12/29/79	Don't Let Go	Isaac Hayes	18	15
12/25/72	1/22/73	Don't Let Me Be Lonely Tonight	James Taylor	13	6
12/24/77	1/28/78	Don't Let Me Be Misunderstood	Santa Esmeralda	20	12
3/1/71	3/15/71	Don't Let The Green Grass Fool You	Wilson Pickett	21	3
7/20/74	8/17/74	Don't Let The Sun Go Down On Me	Elton John	4	11
9/16/78	10/28/78	Don't Look Back	Boston	14	14
5/24/71	7/12/71	Don't Pull Your Love	Hamilton, Joe Frank & Reynolds	3	12
2/14/72	2/21/72	Don't Say You Don't Remember	Beverly Bremers	11	6
7/30/77	9/17/77	Don't Stop	Fleetwood Mac	8	17
9/4/76	9/25/76	Don't Stop Believin'	Olivia Newton-John	27	6
4/13/70	4/20/70	Don't Stop Now	Eddie Holman	37	2
9/29/79	10/27/79	Don't Stop `Til You Get Enough	Michael Jackson	7	20
11/25/78	1/27/79	(Our Love) Don't Throw It All Away	Andy Gibb	11	17
11/9/70	11/16/70	Don't Try To Lay No Boogie Woogie On The "King Of Rock & Roll"	Crow	16	3
10/25/71	11/8/71	Don't Wanna Live Inside Myself	Bee Gees	18	4
8/27/77	10/15/77	Don't Worry Baby	B.J. Thomas	19	12
6/1/74	6/15/74	Don't You Worry 'Bout A Thing	Stevie Wonder	11	3
1/12/74	2/23/74	Doo Doo Doo Doo Doo (Heartbreaker)	Rolling Stones	13	8
10/9/76	11/6/76	Dose Of Rock 'N' Roll, A	Ringo Starr	20	9
5/24/71	6/28/71	Double Barrel	Dave & Ansil Collins	4	8

Debut	Peak	Title	Artist	Pos	Wks
5/3/71	6/14/71	Double Lovin'	Osmonds	5	9
11/4/78	12/2/78	Double Vision	Foreigner	9	20
1/17/72	2/28/72	Down By The Lazy River	Osmonds	2	16
11/10/69	12/8/69	Down On The Corner	Creedence Clearwater Revival	3	10
6/21/71	7/26/71	Draggin' The Line	Tommy James	1	10
3/29/71	4/12/71	Dream Baby (How Long Must I Dream)	Glen Campbell	19	4
2/7/76	3/20/76	Dream On	Aerosmith	2	18
10/13/79	12/8/79	Dream Police	Cheap Trick	8	19
2/14/76	3/27/76	Dream Weaver	Gary Wright	4	17
12/11/76	1/29/77	Dreamboat Annie	Heart	8	15
11/24/79	12/15/79	Dreaming	Blondie	23	12
4/30/77	6/4/77	Dreams	Fleetwood Mac	7	18
1/29/73	2/5/73	Dreidel	Don McLean	21	2
4/9/73	5/21/73	Drift Away	Dobie Gray	5	10
9/22/79	10/20/79	Driver's Seat	Sniff 'n' the Tears	21	9
12/27/71	1/31/72	Drowning In The Sea Of Love	Joe Simon	7	10
2/12/73	2/26/73	Dueling Banjos	Eric Weissberg & Steve Mandell	2	8
5/20/78	6/10/78	Dukey Stick	George Duke	24	11
3/18/78	5/13/78	Dust In The Wind	Kansas	6	22
11/3/73	12/8/73	D'yer Mak'er	Led Zeppelin	6	12
8/2/75	8/23/75	Dynomite—Part I	Bazuka	8	6
9/7/74	9/28/74	Earache My Eye	Cheech & Chong	1	11
11/17/69	12/15/69	Early In The Morning	Vanity Fare	16	9
7/30/77	8/27/77	Easy	Commodores	27	9
3/2/70	4/6/70	Easy Come, Easy Go	Bobby Sherman	8	9
3/25/78	5/6/78	Ebony Eyes	Bob Welch	10	14
3/15/71	4/12/71	Eighteen	Alice Cooper	2	8
10/12/70	11/2/70	El Condor Pasa	Simon & Garfunkel	17	5
11/6/72	11/6/72	Elected	Alice Cooper	26	1
2/22/75	3/29/75	Emma	Hot Chocolate	3	14
1/14/78	4/15/78	Emotion	Samantha Sang	1	26
3/9/74	3/9/74	Energy Crisis '74	Dickie Goodman	12	3
11/16/70	11/16/70	Engine Number 9	Wilson Pickett	26	1
1/8/77	3/5/77	Enjoy Yourself	Jacksons	12	15
4/27/74	5/4/74	Entertainer, The	Marvin Hamlisch	3	8
3/23/74	4/13/74	Eres Tu (Touch The Wind)	Mocedades	5	7
12/1/79	1/12/80	Escape (The Pina Colada Song)	Rupert Holmes	1	20
11/2/74	12/7/74	Everlasting Love	Carl Carlton	8	12
8/12/78	9/16/78	Everlasting Love, An	Andy Gibb	11	14
4/17/72	4/24/72	Every Day Of My Life	Bobby Vinton	29	2
2/10/79	3/10/79	Every 1's A Winner	Hot Chocolate	20	9
3/17/79	4/14/79	Every Time I Think Of You	Babys	20	12
9/4/72	10/23/72	Everybody Plays The Fool	Main Ingredient	1	11
10/18/71	11/22/71	Everybody's Everything	Santana	8	8
7/27/70	7/27/70	Everybody's Got The Right To Love	Supremes	31	2

Debut	Peak	Title	Artist	Pos	Wks
4/6/70	4/27/70	Everybody's Out Of Town	B.J. Thomas	32	4
2/7/72	2/21/72	Everything I Own	Bread	7	8
4/20/70	5/25/70	Everything Is Beautiful	Ray Stevens	6	12
2/16/70	3/16/70	Evil Ways	Santana	14	8
12/27/75	2/14/76	Evil Woman	Electric Light Orchestra	6	17
11/10/69	12/22/69	Evil Woman Don't Play Your Games With Me	Crow	6	11
3/29/75	4/12/75	Express	B.T. Express	16	3
8/23/75	9/13/75	Fallin' In Love	Hamilton, Joe Frank & Reynolds	1	14
9/20/75	10/18/75	Fame	David Bowie	3	15
11/1/71	12/6/71	Family Affair	Sly & The Family Stone	1	12
3/27/72	5/1/72	Family Of Man, The	Three Dog Night	6	10
1/10/76	2/21/76	Fanny (Be Tender With My Love)	Bee Gees	9	17
12/16/78	1/20/79	Fat Bottomed Girls	Queen	20	11
10/4/75	10/18/75	Feel Like Makin' Love	Bad Company	7	4
8/3/74	8/24/74	Feel Like Makin' Love	Roberta Flack	4	11
6/11/73	8/25/73	Feelin' Stronger Every Day	Chicago	4	16
11/15/75	12/13/75	Feelings	Morris Albert	1	18
4/16/77	6/25/77	Feels Like The First Time	Foreigner	3	20
5/27/78	6/24/78	Feels So Good	Chuck Mangione	4	18
9/18/76	10/23/76	Fernando	ABBA	14	11
2/11/78	3/18/78	Ffun	Con Funk Shun	27	9
8/7/76	9/25/76	Fifth Of Beethoven, A	Walter Murphy & the Big Apple Band	4	26
1/10/76	2/7/76	50 Ways To Leave Your Lover	Paul Simon	1	20
9/20/75	10/4/75	Fight The Power Part 1	Isley Brothers	11	3
2/15/75	3/22/75	Fire	Ohio Players	4	14
2/3/79	3/31/79	Fire	Pointer Sisters	2	21
9/28/70	11/2/70	Fire And Rain	James Taylor	2	10
1/17/72	1/17/72	Fire And Water	Wilson Pickett	31	1
9/29/79	10/20/79	Firecracker	Mass Production	32	7
3/5/77	4/16/77	First Cut Is The Deepest, The	Rod Stewart	20	11
3/20/72	4/10/72	First Time Ever I Saw Your Face, The	Roberta Flack	1	12
11/9/70	11/30/70	5-10-15-20 (25-30 Years Of Love)	Presidents	11	6
3/4/78	5/20/78	Flash Light	Parliament	3	23
8/6/77	9/24/77	Float On	Floaters	23	11
2/21/72	3/13/72	Floy Joy	Supremes	14	6
12/27/75	2/7/76	Fly Away	John Denver	19	10
1/1/77	3/5/77	Fly Like An Eagle	Steve Miller	2	23
11/22/75	12/13/75	Fly, Robin, Fly	Silver Convention	8	15
7/29/78	8/19/78	Follow You Follow Me	Genesis	32	8
6/11/73	6/11/73	Fool	Elvis Presley	17	2
9/23/78	10/14/78	Fool (If You Think It's Over)	Chris Rea	26	10
5/15/76	6/12/76	Fool To Cry	Rolling Stones	16	9

Debut	Peak	Title	Artist	Pos	Wks
4/17/76	6/19/76	Fooled Around And Fell In Love	Elvin Bishop	4	15
2/8/71	3/15/71	For All We Know	Carpenters	4	9
12/21/70	1/4/71	For The Good Times	Ray Price	14	4
3/30/70	5/11/70	For The Love Of Him	Bobbi Martin	8	12
6/8/74	6/22/74	For The Love Of Money	O'Jays	6	6
10/27/69	12/8/69	Fortunate Son	Creedence Clearwater Revival	3	12
11/29/75	1/10/76	Fox On The Run	Sweet	2	23
4/16/73	5/28/73	Frankenstein	Edgar Winter Group	1	11
10/16/72	11/6/72	Freddie's Dead (Theme From "Superfly")	Curtis Mayfield	4	8
3/8/71	3/22/71	Free	Chicago	13	5
2/12/77	3/19/77	Free	Deniece Williams	27	9
12/4/76	1/8/77	Free Bird	Lynyrd Skynyrd	10	12
9/15/73	10/27/73	Free Ride	Edgar Winter Group	4	13
4/12/71	4/19/71	Friends	Elton John	25	2
6/14/71	7/19/71	Funky Nassau—Part I	Beginning Of The End	9	7
11/27/72	1/8/73	Funny Face	Donna Fargo	5	9
3/4/78	3/18/78	Galaxy	War	37	5
12/7/70	1/25/71	Games	Redeye	12	6
9/25/72	11/6/72	Garden Party	Rick Nelson	2	9
6/19/76	8/21/76	Get Closer	Seals & Crofts	2	18
12/23/78	1/27/79	Get Down	Gene Chandler	19	15
6/25/73	7/30/73	Get Down	Gilbert O'Sullivan	2	11
9/6/75	9/27/75	Get Down Tonight	KC & the Sunshine Band	1	21
5/24/71	7/19/71	Get It On	Chase	5	11
8/26/78	11/25/78	Get Off	Foxy	6	28
10/2/72	10/16/72	Get On The Good Foot-Part 1	James Brown	17	4
5/20/78	6/3/78	Get On Up	Tyrone Davis	32	6
5/4/70	6/15/70	Get Ready	Rare Earth	1	11
5/1/76	7/3/76	Get Up And Boogie (That's Right)	Silver Convention	2	17
9/11/76	10/9/76	Getaway	Earth, Wind & Fire	23	8
6/16/79	7/28/79	Getting Closer	Wings	20	13
5/18/70	7/6/70	Gimme Dat Ding	Pipkins	7	10
6/3/78	7/15/78	Girl Calling	Chocolate Milk	23	12
8/4/79	8/25/79	Girl Of My Dreams	Bram Tchaikovsky	25	8
12/24/77	1/14/78	Girls' School	Wings	27	8
7/30/77	8/20/77	Give A Little Bit	Supertramp	25	8
5/21/73	6/25/73	Give It To Me	J. Geils Band	17	7
2/2/70	3/9/70	Give Me Just A Little More Time	Chairmen of the Board	4	9
5/14/73	7/2/73	Give Me Love (Give Me Peace On Earth)	George Harrison	2	10
2/12/73	2/19/73	Give Me Your Love	Barbara Mason	24	3
5/3/71	5/24/71	Give More Power To The People	Chi-Lites	17	5
6/18/73	7/2/73	Give Your Baby A Standing Ovation	Dells	26	3

Debut	Peak	Title	Artist	Pos	Wks
4/2/77	4/30/77	Gloria	Enchantment	34	6
2/28/72	3/20/72	Glory Bound	Grass Roots	9	8
8/28/72	10/9/72	Go All The Way	Raspberries	3	10
8/9/71	9/13/71	Go Away Little Girl	Donny Osmond	1	13
1/22/77	3/12/77	Go Your Own Way	Fleetwood Mac	9	15
10/12/70	10/26/70	God, Love And Rock & Roll	Teegarden & Van Winkle	16	4
6/30/79	8/18/79	Gold	John Stewart	12	16
1/17/76	2/28/76	Golden Years	David Bowie	35	12
7/24/72	8/7/72	Gone	Joey Heatherton	23	4
12/3/77	12/17/77	Gone Too Far	England Dan & John Ford Coley	39	3
4/23/77	5/28/77	Gonna Fly Now	Bill Conti	1	18
9/29/79	11/3/79	Good Girls Don't	Knack	7	18
6/1/70	7/6/70	Good Morning Freedom	Daybreak	19	7
10/2/72	11/6/72	Good Time Charlie's Got The Blues	Danny O'Keefe	9	8
7/7/79	9/1/79	Good Times	Chic	2	20
4/15/78	5/13/78	Goodbye Girl	David Gates	13	15
9/8/79	10/6/79	Goodbye Stranger	Supertramp	15	16
7/31/72	8/28/72	Goodbye To Love	Carpenters	7	8
10/27/73	12/22/73	Goodbye Yellow Brick Road	Elton John	1	16
3/24/79	5/19/79	Goodnight Tonight	Wings	9	20
12/2/78	2/17/79	Got To Be Real	Cheryl Lynn	13	21
11/8/71	12/6/71	Got To Be There	Michael Jackson	4	12
6/5/76	7/10/76	Got To Get You Into My Life	Beatles	1	17
8/12/78	9/16/78	Got To Get You Into My Life	Earth, Wind & Fire	17	15
5/7/77	6/4/77	Got To Give It Up (Pt. I)	Marvin Gaye	20	11
2/9/70	3/9/70	Gotta Get Back To You	Tommy James & the Shondells	19	6
2/23/70	3/16/70	Gotta Hold On To This Feeling	Jr. Walker & the All Stars	17	6
7/8/78	8/12/78	Grease	Frankie Valli	3	21
9/28/70	10/19/70	Green-Eyed Lady	Sugarloaf	2	11
4/29/78	6/17/78	Groove Line, The	Heatwave	6	23
1/18/71	2/8/71	Groove Me	King Floyd	15	6
8/10/70	9/7/70	Groovy Situation	Gene Chandler	6	10
3/6/76	3/13/76	Grow Some Funk Of Your Own	Elton John	33	5
8/7/72	8/28/72	Guitar Man, The	Bread	10	9
7/23/73	9/1/73	Gypsy Man	War	11	11
10/19/70	11/16/70	Gypsy Woman	Brian Hyland	2	10
10/4/71	11/1/71	Gypsys, Tramps & Thieves	Cher	2	10
9/1/73	10/6/73	Half-Breed	Cher	1	15
12/8/79	12/29/79	Half The Way	Crystal Gayle	22	10
7/20/70	8/31/70	Hand Me Down World	Guess Who	7	9
7/23/77	9/10/77	Handy Man	James Taylor	3	16

Debut	Peak	Title	Artist	Pos	Wks
8/10/74	8/31/74	Hang On In There Baby	Johnny Bristol	12	5
2/1/71	2/15/71	Hang On To Your Life	Guess Who	15	5
6/12/72	8/14/72	Happiest Girl In The Whole U.S.A., The	Donna Fargo	11	13
7/31/72	8/21/72	Happy	Rolling Stones	17	4
5/1/76	6/5/76	Happy Days	Pratt & McClain	3	13
1/22/77	3/12/77	Hard Luck Woman	Kiss	7	14
1/18/71	2/22/71	Have You Ever Seen The Rain	Creedence Clearwater Revival	4	10
1/25/75	3/15/75	Have You Never Been Mellow	Olivia Newton-John	1	22
11/1/71	12/13/71	Have You Seen Her	Chi-Lites	1	13
6/8/74	6/22/74	Haven't Got Time For The Pain	Carly Simon	21	5
8/17/74	9/7/74	(You're) Having My Baby	Paul Anka with Odia Coates	1	14
11/23/70	12/21/70	He Ain't Heavy... He's My Brother	Neil Diamond	12	6
1/26/70	2/16/70	He Ain't Heavy, He's My Brother	Hollies	13	10
3/29/75	5/10/75	He Don't Love You (Like I Love You)	Tony Orlando & Dawn	4	16
12/1/79	1/12/80	Head Games	Foreigner	16	12
5/21/77	6/25/77	Heard It In A Love Song	Marshall Tucker Band	22	11
3/31/79	6/2/79	Heart Of Glass	Blondie	2	26
2/21/72	3/13/72	Heart Of Gold	Neil Young	1	11
7/21/79	8/4/79	Heart Of The Night	Poco	33	7
9/29/79	11/17/79	Heartache Tonight	Eagles	4	22
9/22/73	10/20/73	Heartbeat—It's A Lovebeat	DeFranco Family featuring Tony DeFranco	1	17
10/18/75	11/15/75	Heat Wave	Linda Ronstadt	5	15
10/26/70	11/16/70	Heaven Help Us All	Stevie Wonder	6	8
11/17/69	12/15/69	Heaven Knows	Grass Roots	22	8
2/10/79	3/24/79	Heaven Knows	Donna Summer with Brooklyn Dreams	8	19
7/31/76	9/11/76	Heaven Must Be Missing An Angel (Part 1)	Tavares	20	12
10/13/79	10/27/79	Heaven Must Have Sent You	Bonnie Pointer	33	8
10/22/77	12/31/77	Heaven On The 7th Floor	Paul Nicholas	4	21
11/26/77	12/10/77	Heaven's Just A Sin Away	Kendalls	32	6
11/24/73	1/5/74	Helen Wheels	Paul McCartney & Wings	13	11
10/20/73	12/15/73	Hello, It's Me	Todd Rundgren	1	16
11/27/76	12/18/76	Hello Old Friend	Eric Clapton	31	7
5/7/77	6/4/77	Hello Stranger	Yvonne Elliman	28	8
10/1/77	12/10/77	Help Is On Its Way	Little River Band	19	14
5/18/74	6/29/74	Help Me	Joni Mitchell	6	11
2/22/71	3/22/71	Help Me Make It Through The Night	Sammi Smith	10	7
2/26/77	3/26/77	Here Come Those Tears Again	Jackson Browne	31	7
6/14/71	7/5/71	Here Comes That Rainy Day Feeling Again	Fortunes	3	6

Debut	Peak	Title	Artist	Pos	Wks
4/12/71	5/17/71	Here Comes The Sun	Richie Havens	5	9
8/18/73	9/1/73	Here I Am (Come And Take Me)	Al Green	18	4
11/26/77	1/14/78	Here You Come Again	Dolly Parton	3	17
4/21/79	5/26/79	He's The Greatest Dancer	Sister Sledge	17	15
12/13/71	1/17/72	Hey Big Brother	Rare Earth	13	10
12/10/77	1/21/78	Hey Deanie	Shaun Cassidy	6	19
12/6/71	12/27/71	Hey Girl	Donny Osmond	4	11
3/30/70	5/11/70	Hey Lawdy Mama	Steppenwolf	13	9
5/25/70	6/22/70	Hey, Mister Sun	Bobby Sherman	14	8
12/29/69	2/2/70	Hey There Lonely Girl	Eddie Holman	3	13
6/21/75	7/12/75	Hey You	Bachman-Turner Overdrive	9	7
8/17/70	8/31/70	Hi-De-Ho	Blood, Sweat & Tears	11	6
5/14/77	6/18/77	High School Dance	Sylvers	17	12
5/31/71	7/12/71	High Time We Went	Joe Cocker	8	9
6/25/77	8/20/77	Higher And Higher	Rita Coolidge	2	20
9/1/73	9/29/73	Higher Ground	Stevie Wonder	9	11
3/30/70	6/1/70	Hitchin' A Ride	Vanity Fare	1	16
5/7/73	6/4/73	Hocus Pocus	Focus	5	8
7/17/72	8/7/72	Hold Her Tight	Osmonds	11	5
12/23/78	2/3/79	Hold The Line	Toto	6	19
7/17/72	8/28/72	Hold Your Head Up	Argent	4	10
10/13/69	11/17/69	Holly Holy	Neil Diamond	2	14
9/23/78	10/21/78	Hollywood Nights	Bob Seger & the Silver Bullet Band	22	12
1/12/70	2/23/70	Honey Come Back	Glen Campbell	22	8
9/4/72	9/25/72	Honky Cat	Elton John	9	6
3/2/74	3/30/74	Hooked On A Feeling	Blue Swede	1	15
8/12/78	9/23/78	Hopelessly Devoted To You	Olivia Newton-John	7	16
3/6/72	3/27/72	Horse With No Name, A	America	1	11
7/29/78	9/30/78	Hot Blooded	Foreigner	3	30
9/30/78	11/25/78	Hot Child In The City	Nick Gilder	1	24
4/8/78	5/6/78	Hot Legs	Rod Stewart	23	8
12/4/76	2/12/77	Hot Line	Sylvers	1	26
5/3/71	5/17/71	Hot Love	T. Rex	24	3
5/5/79	6/16/79	Hot Stuff	Donna Summer	1	24
8/11/79	9/29/79	Hot Summer Nights	Night	17	13
3/19/77	5/7/77	Hotel California	Eagles	3	18
2/9/70	3/9/70	House Of The Rising Sun	Frijid Pink	8	11
6/5/72	6/19/72	How Can I Be Sure	David Cassidy	16	3
1/12/70	1/26/70	How Can I Forget	Marvin Gaye	28	3
7/30/73	9/1/73	How Can I Tell Her	Lobo	26	8
6/28/71	8/2/71	How Can You Mend A Broken Heart	Bee Gees	1	10
10/29/77	12/24/77	How Deep Is Your Love	Bee Gees	1	31
6/12/72	8/14/72	How Do You Do	Mouth & MacNeal	6	11
4/12/75	5/10/75	How Long	Ace	8	15
11/4/78	12/9/78	How Much I Feel	Ambrosia	8	17
7/23/77	9/17/77	How Much Love	Leo Sayer	5	16
9/6/75	9/20/75	How Sweet It Is (To Be Loved By You)	James Taylor	16	3

Debut	Peak	Title	Artist	Pos	Wks
12/23/78	1/20/79	How You Gonna See Me Now	Alice Cooper	26	11
4/27/70	5/11/70	Hum A Song (From Your Heart)	Lulu	28	3
3/19/73	3/19/73	Hummingbird	Seals & Crofts	19	1
1/24/76	2/7/76	Hurricane (Part I)	Bob Dylan	38	3
8/25/73	9/22/73	Hurt, The	Cat Stevens	11	9
1/24/72	2/14/72	Hurting Each Other	Carpenters	1	11
6/21/75	7/12/75	Hustle, The	Van McCoy with the Soul City Symphony	4	19
8/10/70	9/21/70	I (Who Have Nothing)	Tom Jones	4	10
9/6/71	9/13/71	I Ain't Got Time Anymore	Glass Bottle	17	3
3/8/71	4/19/71	I Am... I Said	Neil Diamond	2	10
3/8/75	4/19/75	I Am Love (Parts I & II)	Jackson 5	8	13
10/23/72	12/11/72	I Am Woman	Helen Reddy	1	14
10/16/72	11/13/72	I Believe In Music	Gallery	14	7
7/16/73	9/1/73	I Believe In You (You Believe In Me)	Johnnie Taylor	10	10
11/30/74	12/21/74	I Can Help	Billy Swan	4	14
10/16/72	11/13/72	I Can See Clearly Now	Johnny Nash	1	11
2/7/72	3/6/72	I Can't Help Myself (Sugar Pie, Honey Bunch)	Donnie Elbert	12	8
5/8/72	6/12/72	(Last Night) I Didn't Get To Sleep At All	Fifth Dimension	6	11
9/29/79	10/27/79	I Do Love You	GQ	26	10
4/5/71	4/26/71	I Don't Blame You At All	Smokey Robinson & the Miracles	12	5
5/17/71	6/14/71	I Don't Know How To Love Him	Helen Reddy	6	6
12/30/78	2/17/79	I Don't Know If It's Right	Evelyn "Champagne" King	23	14
5/10/75	5/24/75	I Don't Like To Sleep Alone	Paul Anka with Odia Coates	12	3
7/10/72	8/14/72	(If Loving You Is Wrong) I Don't Want To Be Right	Luther Ingram	3	10
6/21/71	7/12/71	I Don't Want To Do Wrong	Gladys Knight & The Pips	18	5
10/1/77	11/12/77	I Feel Love	Donna Summer	4	16
8/9/71	8/9/71	I Feel The Earth Move	Carole King	15	3
11/12/77	12/3/77	I Go Crazy	Paul Davis	31	5
10/6/73	12/8/73	I Got A Name	Jim Croce	1	18
4/7/79	5/12/79	I Got My Mind Made Up (You Can Get It Girl)	Instant Funk	26	12
2/14/72	4/10/72	I Gotcha	Joe Tex	3	13
12/14/70	1/18/71	I Hear You Knocking	Dave Edmunds	1	12
9/14/74	10/5/74	I Honestly Love You	Olivia Newton-John	1	16
7/20/70	8/24/70	I Just Can't Help Believing	B.J. Thomas	2	12
4/21/79	5/5/79	I Just Fall In Love Again	Anne Murray	33	7
11/11/78	12/30/78	I Just Wanna Stop	Gino Vannelli	9	18
6/11/77	8/13/77	I Just Want To Be Your Everything	Andy Gibb	1	25
7/26/71	8/30/71	I Just Want To Celebrate	Rare Earth	8	10

Debut	Peak	Title	Artist	Pos	Wks
10/15/77	11/19/77	I Just Want To Make Love To You	Foghat	15	12
11/17/79	12/8/79	I Know A Heartache When I See One	Jennifer Warnes	32	6
2/5/77	4/30/77	I Like Dreamin'	Kenny Nolan	7	18
8/26/78	10/14/78	I Like Girls	Fatback Band	21	13
1/8/77	1/22/77	I Like To Do It	KC & the Sunshine Band	36	4
1/19/74	2/23/74	I Love	Tom T. Hall	25	6
12/27/75	1/31/76	I Love Music (Part 1)	O'Jays	12	14
12/9/78	1/27/79	I Love The Nightlife (Disco 'Round)	Alicia Bridges	8	26
4/12/71	5/10/71	I Love You For All Seasons	Fuzz	12	6
7/24/76	8/14/76	I Need To Be In Love	Carpenters	35	5
5/29/72	7/3/72	I Need You	America	7	7
10/30/76	12/4/76	I Never Cry	Alice Cooper	29	9
12/27/75	12/27/75	I Only Have Eyes For You	Art Garfunkel	43	1
9/4/76	10/30/76	I Only Want To Be With You	Bay City Rollers	2	23
3/29/71	4/19/71	I Play And Sing	Dawn	3	7
1/11/71	2/8/71	I Really Don't Want To Know	Elvis Presley	7	7
5/8/72	6/5/72	I Saw The Light	Todd Rundgren	13	7
8/24/74	9/14/74	I Shot The Sheriff	Eric Clapton	2	12
12/29/69	1/5/70	I Started Loving You Again	Al Martino	38	2
10/19/70	11/2/70	I Think I Love You	Partridge Family	1	12
6/19/72	7/24/72	I Wanna Be Where You Are	Michael Jackson	11	7
12/4/72	1/15/73	I Wanna Be With You	Raspberries	16	9
4/16/77	5/21/77	I Wanna Get Next To You	Rose Royce	22	10
6/26/76	7/17/76	I Want You	Marvin Gaye	30	6
11/17/69	12/15/69	I Want You Back	Jackson 5	2	12
5/26/79	7/7/79	I Want You To Want Me	Cheap Trick	2	24
3/17/79	4/21/79	I Want Your Love	Chic	13	17
6/30/79	8/4/79	I Was Made For Lovin' You	Kiss	15	18
1/20/79	3/31/79	I Will Survive	Gloria Gaynor	1	27
12/11/76	2/12/77	I Wish	Stevie Wonder	5	17
8/9/71	9/20/71	I Woke Up In Love This Morning	Partridge Family	3	10
5/25/74	6/8/74	I Won't Last A Day Without You	Carpenters	15	3
10/1/77	11/5/77	I Wouldn't Want To Be Like You	Alan Parsons	21	10
12/6/75	1/31/76	I Write The Songs	Barry Manilow	1	24
11/29/71	1/17/72	I'd Like To Teach The World To Sing (In Perfect Harmony)	New Seekers	9	12
10/23/72	11/27/72	I'd Love You To Want Me	Lobo	2	8
7/10/76	9/11/76	I'd Really Love To See You Tonight	England Dan & John Ford Coley	3	19
3/22/71	4/26/71	If	Bread	2	10

Debut	Peak	Title	Artist	Pos	Wks
3/25/78	5/6/78	If I Can't Have You	Yvonne Elliman	9	16
10/9/72	11/27/72	If I Could Reach You	Fifth Dimension	7	10
12/15/69	2/9/70	If I Never Knew Your Name	Vic Dana	7	13
12/21/70	1/25/71	If I Were Your Woman	Gladys Knight & The Pips	4	10
3/4/78	3/4/78	If It Don't Fit, Don't Force It	Kellee Patterson	45	2
5/31/71	6/28/71	If Not For You	Olivia Newton-John	2	7
1/18/71	2/22/71	If You Could Read My Mind	Gordon Lightfoot	2	10
11/13/72	12/4/72	If You Don't Know Me By Now	Harold Melvin & the Blue Notes	7	10
8/14/76	9/4/76	If You Know What I Mean	Neil Diamond	28	7
8/21/76	9/18/76	If You Leave Me Now	Chicago	1	20
6/29/74	7/6/74	If You Love Me (Let Me Know)	Olivia Newton-John	7	6
9/20/71	10/18/71	If You Really Love Me	Stevie Wonder	4	9
6/18/73	6/25/73	If You Want Me To Stay	Sly & the Family Stone	22	9
11/24/73	12/22/73	If You're Ready (Come Go With Me)	Staple Singers	24	11
7/2/73	7/2/73	I'll Always Love My Mama (Part 1)	Intruders	29	2
10/16/72	11/20/72	I'll Be Around	Spinners	2	8
7/3/76	7/31/76	I'll Be Good To You	Brothers Johnson	14	10
9/14/70	10/12/70	I'll Be There	Jackson 5	1	13
4/20/74	5/4/74	I'll Have To Say I Love You In A Song	Jim Croce	8	4
4/12/71	6/7/71	I'll Meet You Halfway	Partridge Family	5	11
12/22/69	2/2/70	I'll Never Fall In Love Again	Dionne Warwick	6	10
8/25/79	10/20/79	I'll Never Love This Way Again	Dionne Warwick	5	18
5/8/72	6/5/72	I'll Take You There	Staple Singers	1	9
10/4/71	10/18/71	I'm Comin' Home	Tommy James	12	4
5/7/73	6/18/73	I'm Doin' Fine Now	New York City	15	10
7/3/76	8/14/76	I'm Easy	Keith Carradine	4	14
11/25/78	12/30/78	I'm Every Woman	Chaka Khan	23	13
5/7/73	6/25/73	I'm Gonna Love You Just A Little More Baby	Barry White	2	10
6/4/77	7/23/77	I'm In You	Peter Frampton	2	16
2/12/73	3/19/73	I'm Just A Singer (In A Rock And Roll Band)	Moody Blues	7	8
8/10/74	9/14/74	I'm Leaving It (All) Up To You	Donny & Marie Osmond	5	11
8/17/70	9/28/70	(I Know) I'm Losing You	Rare Earth	5	10
7/5/75	8/9/75	I'm Not In Love	10cc	2	14
12/14/70	12/14/70	I'm Not My Brother's Keeper	Flaming Ember	30	1
12/27/75	12/27/75	I'm On Fire	5000 Volts	37	2
2/24/79	3/17/79	I'm So Into You	Peabo Bryson	35	5
9/27/75	11/1/75	I'm Sorry	John Denver	4	14
7/24/72	9/11/72	I'm Still In Love With You	Al Green	2	10

Debut	Peak	Title	Artist	Pos	Wks
11/13/72	12/18/72	I'm Stone In Love With You	Stylistics	10	10
6/22/74	7/13/74	I'm The Leader Of The Gang	Brownsville Station	11	5
6/7/71	7/19/71	I'm The Only One	Lobo	11	8
4/23/77	6/11/77	I'm Your Boogie Man	KC & the Sunshine Band	2	20
4/29/78	6/17/78	Imaginary Lover	Atlanta Rhythm Section	9	17
10/18/71	11/15/71	Imagine	John Lennon	2	9
12/7/70	1/18/71	Immigrant Song	Led Zeppelin	3	10
6/12/72	6/19/72	Immigration Man	Graham Nash & David Crosby	27	2
9/22/73	10/6/73	In The Midnight Hour	Cross Country	32	5
4/14/79	5/12/79	In The Mood	Tyrone Davis	38	8
1/15/77	1/29/77	In The Mood	Henhouse Five Plus Too	27	4
4/7/79	5/12/79	In The Navy	Village People	10	19
3/27/72	4/24/72	In The Rain	Dramatics	7	8
7/20/70	8/31/70	In The Summertime	Mungo Jerry	4	11
5/31/71	7/5/71	Indian Reservation	Raiders	5	10
9/7/70	10/4/70	Indiana Wants Me	R. Dean Taylor	4	9
10/18/71	11/15/71	Inner City Blues (Make Me Wanna Holler)	Marvin Gaye	6	7
2/23/70	3/16/70	Instant Karma (We All Shine On)	John Lennon	2	11
5/22/76	6/5/76	I.O.U.	Jimmy Dean	21	5
8/4/79	9/8/79	Is She Really Going Out With Him	Joe Jackson	8	15
10/11/75	11/15/75	Island Girl	Elton John	1	19
11/5/77	12/17/77	Isn't It Time	Babys	8	16
5/22/72	6/5/72	Isn't Life Strange	Moody Blues	16	4
5/3/71	6/7/71	It Don't Come Easy	Ringo Starr	2	8
10/4/70	10/26/70	It Don't Matter To Me	Bread	3	8
9/25/72	12/25/72	It Never Rains In Southern California	Albert Hammond	3	17
11/1/75	11/8/75	It Only Takes A Minute	Tavares	16	3
5/7/73	5/14/73	It Sure Took A Long, Long Time	Lobo	20	2
6/3/78	7/8/78	It's A Heartache	Bonnie Tyler	5	17
10/23/76	11/20/76	It's A Long Way There	Little River Band	31	6
4/19/75	5/24/75	It's A Miracle	Barry Manilow	1	16
5/18/70	7/6/70	It's All In The Game	Four Tops	16	9
9/17/77	10/29/77	It's Ecstasy When You Lay Down Next To Me	Barry White	17	12
5/8/72	6/12/72	It's Going To Take Some Time	Carpenters	9	8
9/4/76	10/2/76	It's O.K.	Beach Boys	23	7
12/13/71	1/10/72	It's One Of Those Nights (Yes Love)	Partridge Family	7	9
10/23/76	11/13/76	It's Only Love	ZZ Top	31	5
10/12/70	11/2/70	It's Only Make Believe	Glen Campbell	18	5
8/3/74	9/21/74	It's Only Rock 'N Roll (But I Like It)	Rolling Stones	14	3

Debut	Peak	Title	Artist	Pos	Wks
6/25/77	7/30/77	It's Sad To Belong	England Dan & John Ford Coley	15	11
11/12/77	1/7/78	It's So Easy	Linda Ronstadt	6	16
5/24/71	6/21/71	It's Too Late	Carole King	1	14
3/4/78	4/8/78	It's You That I Need	Enchantment	25	12
6/5/72	6/12/72	I've Been Lonely For So Long	Frederick Knight	26	2
9/27/71	10/25/71	I've Found Someone Of My Own	Free Movement	2	9
3/12/77	4/23/77	I've Got Love On My Mind	Natalie Cole	14	13
12/22/73	2/23/74	I've Got To Use My Imagination	Gladys Knight & the Pips	11	13
2/4/78	5/13/78	Jack And Jill	Raydio	3	25
4/5/75	5/10/75	Jackie Blue	Ozark Mountain Daredevils	1	16
11/17/69	1/5/70	Jam Up Jelly Tight	Tommy Roe	5	13
1/22/73	2/26/73	Jambalaya (On The Bayou)	Blue Ridge Rangers	14	7
12/8/79	1/19/80	Jane	Jefferson Starship	6	16
10/12/74	11/9/74	Jazzman	Carole King	3	14
11/13/76	12/4/76	Jeans On	David Dundas	34	5
2/23/70	3/2/70	Jennifer Tomkins	Street People	32	3
10/13/73	11/3/73	Jesse	Roberta Flack	31	4
3/2/74	4/20/74	Jet	Paul McCartney & Wings	10	12
5/21/77	7/2/77	Jet Airliner	Steve Miller Band	7	14
1/12/74	3/9/74	Jim Dandy	Black Oak Arkansas	9	10
9/15/73	10/13/73	Jimmy Loves Mary-Anne	Looking Glass	2	11
12/1/69	1/5/70	Jingle Jangle	Archies	8	9
7/26/75	8/23/75	Jive Talkin'	Bee Gees	2	17
9/28/70	10/12/70	Joanne	Michael Nesmith	13	5
3/1/71	3/15/71	Jody's Got Your Girl And Gone	Johnnie Taylor	22	3
8/21/72	9/4/72	Join Together	Who	21	3
11/24/73	12/29/73	Joker, The	Steve Miller Band	1	14
1/31/72	2/21/72	Joy	Apollo 100	4	11
3/22/71	4/19/71	Joy To The World	Three Dog Night	1	13
8/24/70	9/21/70	Julie, Do Ya Love Me	Bobby Sherman	3	9
3/16/74	3/30/74	Jungle Boogie	Kool & the Gang	12	4
3/13/72	3/27/72	Jungle Fever	Chakachas	6	7
9/3/77	10/15/77	Jungle Love	Steve Miller Band	23	11
11/23/74	12/21/74	Junior's Farm	Paul McCartney & Wings	7	13
2/28/76	4/3/76	Junk Food Junkie	Larry Groce	21	10
7/2/77	8/27/77	Just A Song Before I Go	Crosby, Stills & Nash	11	14
4/20/74	5/4/74	Just Don't Want To Be Lonely	Main Ingredient	14	4
2/22/71	3/22/71	Just My Imagination	Temptations	1	10
9/17/77	11/5/77	Just Remember I Love You	Firefall	4	15
12/31/77	2/25/78	Just The Way You Are	Billy Joel	2	29
10/16/76	11/20/76	Just To Be Close To You	Commodores	19	10
5/19/79	6/23/79	Just When I Needed You Most	Randy VanWarmer	12	16

Debut	Peak	Title	Artist	Pos	Wks
10/6/73	11/24/73	Just You 'N' Me	Chicago	2	14
9/3/77	10/15/77	Keep It Comin' Love	KC & the Sunshine Band	2	18
4/28/79	6/2/79	Keep On Dancin'	Gary's Gang	23	10
4/27/74	5/4/74	Keep On Singing	Helen Reddy	17	2
8/31/74	8/31/74	Keep On Smilin'	Wet Willie	15	1
9/22/73	10/27/73	Keep On Truckin' (Part 1)	Eddie Kendricks	6	14
12/4/72	1/15/73	Keeper Of The Castle	Four Tops	7	9
2/9/70	3/16/70	Kentucky Rain	Elvis Presley	12	9
4/26/75	5/31/75	Killer Queen	Queen	1	19
2/12/73	3/5/73	Killing Me Softly With His Song	Roberta Flack	1	11
9/24/77	10/29/77	King Is Gone, The	Ronnie McDowell	10	10
6/10/78	7/22/78	King Tut	Steve Martin & the Toot Uncommons	1	21
7/10/76	8/28/76	Kiss And Say Goodbye	Manhattans	23	9
9/2/78	10/21/78	Kiss You All Over	Exile	1	25
3/5/73	3/12/73	Kissing My Love	Bill Withers	20	3
3/17/79	4/28/79	Knock On Wood	Amii Stewart	1	23
11/23/70	12/28/70	Knock Three Times	Dawn	1	13
10/13/73	11/24/73	Knockin' On Heaven's Door	Bob Dylan	19	10
6/4/77	8/13/77	Knowing Me, Knowing You	ABBA	5	19
5/21/73	6/25/73	Kodachrome	Paul Simon	4	13
11/16/74	12/7/74	Kung Fu Fighting	Carl Douglas	1	17
3/8/71	4/5/71	L.A. Goodbye	Ides Of March	5	9
6/15/74	6/29/74	La Grange	ZZ Top	4	10
11/24/69	1/12/70	La La La (If I Had You)	Bobby Sherman	10	10
10/27/79	12/1/79	Ladies Night	Kool & the Gang	8	25
3/3/79	5/5/79	Lady	Little River Band	7	22
12/7/74	2/8/75	Lady	Styx	2	20
3/4/78	4/22/78	Lady Love	Lou Rawls	19	14
3/15/75	4/5/75	Lady Marmalade	Labelle	2	16
6/10/78	7/22/78	Last Dance	Donna Summer	4	33
12/27/75	12/27/75	Last Game Of The Season (A Blind Man In The Bleachers)	David Geddes	32	2
2/23/74	3/23/74	Last Kiss	Wednesday	1	13
2/5/73	3/12/73	Last Song	Edward Bear	3	10
12/21/74	1/11/75	Laughter In The Rain	Neil Sedaka	2	13
6/22/70	8/3/70	Lay A Little Lovin' On Me	Robin McNamara	6	11
5/11/70	6/22/70	Lay Down (Candles In The Rain)	Melanie	5	14
2/11/78	4/29/78	Lay Down Sally	Eric Clapton	8	19
12/2/78	12/30/78	Le Freak	Chic	1	26
8/18/79	9/22/79	Lead Me On	Maxine Nightingale	11	16
5/29/72	7/17/72	Lean On Me	Bill Withers	1	13
11/3/73	12/29/73	Leave Me Alone (Ruby Red Dress)	Helen Reddy	4	15
5/21/73	6/4/73	Leaving Me	Independents	22	4

Debut	Peak	Title	Artist	Pos	Wks
10/13/69	12/1/69	Leaving On A Jet Plane	Peter, Paul & Mary	4	15
7/17/76	8/28/76	Let 'Em In	Wings	2	16
6/12/76	7/24/76	Let Her In	John Travolta	5	15
11/29/71	12/13/71	Let It Be	Joan Baez	17	4
3/9/70	3/30/70	Let It Be	Beatles	1	10
12/15/73	1/12/74	Let Me Be There	Olivia Newton-John	9	12
9/15/73	10/20/73	Let Me In	Osmonds	12	12
10/27/73	12/8/73	Let Me Serenade You	Three Dog Night	11	12
3/27/76	5/15/76	Let Your Love Flow	Bellamy Brothers	3	17
12/21/70	1/25/71	Let Your Love Go	Bread	11	8
11/22/75	12/20/75	Let's Do It Again	Staple Singers	7	11
7/30/73	9/8/73	Let's Get It On	Marvin Gaye	1	15
8/4/79	9/15/79	Let's Go	Cars	5	20
6/4/73	6/18/73	Let's Pretend	Raspberries	21	4
12/20/71	1/24/72	Let's Stay Together	Al Green	2	13
10/12/70	11/16/70	Let's Work Together	Canned Heat	4	11
4/27/70	6/1/70	Letter, The	Joe Cocker	2	10
8/2/71	8/16/71	Liar	Three Dog Night	10	6
4/9/77	6/4/77	Lido Shuffle	Boz Scaggs	2	18
5/21/77	7/9/77	Life In The Fast Lane	Eagles	8	13
10/12/74	11/30/74	Life Is A Rock (But The Radio Rolled Me)	Reunion	1	17
7/29/78	9/16/78	Life's Been Good	Joe Walsh	9	20
5/24/71	6/14/71	Light Sings	Fifth Dimension	16	5
1/31/72	2/28/72	Lion Sleeps Tonight, The	Robert John	3	12
10/2/72	11/6/72	Listen To The Music	Doobie Brothers	6	9
6/28/75	8/9/75	Listen To What The Man Said	Wings	1	17
8/28/76	10/23/76	Little Bit More, A	Dr. Hook	27	11
4/10/72	5/29/72	Little Bitty Pretty One	Jackson 5	4	11
3/30/70	5/18/70	Little Green Bag	George Baker Selection	4	12
1/13/79	2/17/79	Little More Love, A	Olivia Newton-John	6	18
4/2/73	4/23/73	Little Willy	Sweet	5	8
7/2/73	9/1/73	Live And Let Die	Wings	1	14
2/24/79	3/24/79	Livin' It Up (Friday Night)	Bell & James	24	13
11/13/76	12/25/76	Livin' Thing	Electric Light Orchestra	11	14
12/1/73	1/12/74	Living For The City	Stevie Wonder	13	12
6/5/72	7/3/72	Living In A House Divided	Cher	16	6
12/18/72	1/8/73	Living In The Past	Jethro Tull	9	7
4/6/74	5/4/74	Loco-motion, The	Grand Funk	1	14
5/19/79	6/30/79	Logical Song, The	Supertramp	6	23
9/21/70	10/19/70	Lola	Kinks	4	9
4/30/77	6/25/77	Lonely Boy	Andrew Gold	2	18
12/14/70	1/4/71	Lonely Days	Bee Gees	2	9
2/7/76	3/13/76	Lonely Night (Angel Face)	Captain & Tennille	1	20
2/8/75	3/22/75	Lonely People	America	5	14
8/25/79	10/27/79	Lonesome Loser	Little River Band	6	21
5/18/70	6/22/70	Long And Winding Road, The	Beatles	1	13
7/10/72	9/4/72	Long Cool Woman (In A Black Dress)	Hollies	2	12
12/18/72	12/25/72	Long Dark Road	Hollies	26	2

Debut	Peak	Title	Artist	Pos	Wks
3/16/70	4/13/70	Long Lonesome Highway	Michael Parks	9	8
1/7/78	2/25/78	Long, Long Way From Home	Foreigner	16	14
12/15/79	2/2/80	Long Run, The	Eagles	14	14
4/26/75	6/7/75	Long Tall Glasses (I Can Dance)	Leo Sayer	2	15
2/12/77	3/26/77	Long Time	Boston	8	14
5/28/73	7/9/73	Long Train Runnin'	Doobie Brothers	2	11
11/9/74	12/7/74	Longfellow Serenade	Neil Diamond	5	13
10/4/70	10/19/70	Look What They've Done To My Song Ma	New Seekers	7	7
4/10/72	5/22/72	Look What You Done For Me	Al Green	3	10
4/6/74	5/4/74	Lookin' For A Love	Bobby Womack	13	6
8/3/70	9/14/70	Lookin' Out My Back Door	Creedence Clearwater Revival	1	13
12/20/71	1/17/72	Looking For A Love	J. Geils Band	18	7
5/14/77	7/16/77	Looks Like We Made It	Barry Manilow	3	18
3/23/74	4/27/74	Lord's Prayer, The	Sister Janet Mead	2	9
3/20/76	4/17/76	Lorelei	Styx	8	14
1/8/77	2/26/77	Lost Without Your Love	Bread	18	13
1/20/79	2/17/79	Lotta Love	Nicolette Larson	12	14
4/28/79	5/26/79	Love Ballad	George Benson	26	8
11/6/76	12/4/76	Love Ballad	L.T.D.	26	7
2/9/70	3/16/70	Love Grows (Where My Rosemary Goes)	Edison Lighthouse	1	13
4/24/76	6/19/76	Love Hangover	Diana Ross	2	16
4/5/71	5/10/71	Love Her Madly	Doors	4	10
2/7/76	4/3/76	Love Hurts	Nazareth	5	16
11/17/73	12/8/73	Love I Lost (Part 1), The	Harold Melvin & the Blue Notes	21	8
5/8/76	6/26/76	Love In The Shadows	Neil Sedaka	8	12
5/22/76	7/17/76	Love Is Alive	Gary Wright	12	17
10/14/78	11/18/78	Love Is In The Air	John Paul Young	15	14
2/14/76	4/3/76	Love Is The Drug	Roxy Music	32	10
1/22/73	1/29/73	Love Jones	Brighter Side Of Darkness	14	3
6/8/70	7/6/70	Love Land	Charles Wright & the Watts 103rd Street Rhythm Band	13	8
1/31/76	2/28/76	Love Machine (Part 1)	Miracles	16	13
11/20/76	12/25/76	Love Me	Yvonne Elliman	18	9
9/28/74	11/9/74	Love Me For A Reason	Osmonds	7	14
7/12/71	7/12/71	Love Means (You Never Have To Say You're Sorry)	Sounds Of Sunshine	27	2
5/4/70	6/15/70	Love On A Two-Way Street	Moments	5	11
4/6/70	5/18/70	Love Or Let Me Be Lonely	Friends of Distinction	9	12
5/29/76	6/12/76	Love Really Hurts Without You	Billy Ocean	38	3
12/27/75	1/24/76	Love Rollercoaster	Ohio Players	4	19
10/2/76	11/27/76	Love So Right	Bee Gees	14	14
2/23/74	3/16/74	Love Song	Anne Murray	5	9

Debut	Peak	Title	Artist	Pos	Wks
3/1/71	4/5/71	(Where Do I Begin) Love Story	Andy Williams	12	7
2/1/71	3/1/71	Love Story, Theme From	Henry Mancini	3	8
7/19/71	8/9/71	Love The One You're With	Isley Brothers	17	5
12/14/70	1/18/71	Love The One You're With	Stephen Stills	2	10
1/3/76	1/31/76	Love To Love You Baby	Donna Summer	3	13
2/5/73	3/26/73	Love Train	O'Jays	1	11
8/5/78	9/16/78	Love Will Find A Way	Pablo Cruise	6	20
6/14/75	7/5/75	Love Will Keep Us Together	Captain & Tennille	1	25
5/12/79	6/16/79	Love You Inside Out	Bee Gees	9	14
6/1/70	6/29/70	Love You Save, The	Jackson 5	1	13
1/28/78	2/25/78	Lovely Day	Bill Withers	29	9
2/22/71	3/15/71	Love's Lines, Angles And Rhymes	Fifth Dimension	9	6
4/19/71	5/31/71	Love's Made A Fool Of You	Cochise	10	8
8/18/73	9/29/73	Loves Me Like A Rock	Paul Simon	1	13
12/15/73	2/16/74	Love's Theme	Love Unlimited Orchestra	4	15
9/22/79	11/10/79	Lovin', Touchin', Squeezin'	Journey	2	25
3/22/75	4/26/75	Lovin' You	Minnie Riperton	2	13
10/16/72	10/30/72	Loving You Just Crossed My Mind	Sam Neely	26	3
8/28/76	10/2/76	Lowdown	Boz Scaggs	7	14
5/7/77	6/18/77	Lucille	Kenny Rogers	11	13
7/16/77	8/6/77	Luckenbach, Texas (Back To The Basics Of Love)	Waylon Jennings	31	5
10/4/70	11/2/70	Lucretia Mac Evil	Blood, Sweat & Tears	13	7
11/30/74	1/4/75	Lucy In The Sky With Diamonds	Elton John	1	16
5/3/71	5/3/71	Lullaby In The Rain	Happenings	32	1
10/11/75	11/15/75	Lyin' Eyes	Eagles	4	14
1/12/70	2/16/70	Ma Belle Amie	Tee Set	9	11
10/14/78	12/9/78	MacArthur Park	Donna Summer	2	23
9/2/78	10/21/78	Macho Man	Village People	3	38
12/25/76	1/22/77	Mademoiselle	Styx	31	7
8/30/71	9/27/71	Maggie May	Rod Stewart	1	13
6/14/75	6/28/75	Magic	Pilot	2	15
8/28/76	10/9/76	Magic Man	Heart	7	14
8/19/78	10/21/78	Magnet And Steel	Walter Egan	6	19
12/20/75	1/17/76	Mahogany, Theme From (Do You Know Where You're Going To)	Diana Ross	5	14
7/28/79	9/8/79	Main Event/Fight, The	Barbra Streisand	3	18
6/11/77	7/2/77	Mainstreet	Bob Seger	38	4
6/29/70	7/27/70	Make It With You	Bread	1	13
5/11/70	6/22/70	Make Me Smile	Chicago	7	10
5/12/79	6/30/79	Makin' It	David Naughton	2	25
7/14/79	8/25/79	Mama Can't Buy You Love	Elton John	22	14

Debut	Peak	Title	Artist	Pos	Wks
6/1/70	7/6/70	Mama Told Me (Not To Come)	Three Dog Night	2	13
1/18/71	2/15/71	Mama's Pearl	Jackson 5	1	10
11/10/73	12/22/73	Mammy Blue	Stories	15	11
1/4/75	1/25/75	Mandy	Barry Manilow	1	16
6/4/77	8/13/77	Margaritaville	Jimmy Buffett	8	17
8/23/71	9/27/71	Marianne	Stephen Stills	6	9
3/19/73	4/30/73	Masterpiece	Temptations	9	7
2/26/77	4/2/77	Maybe I'm Amazed	Wings	15	10
7/19/71	8/16/71	Maybe Tomorrow	Jackson 5	7	8
1/12/74	1/19/74	Me And Baby Brother	War	39	2
2/8/71	3/8/71	Me And Bobby McGee	Janis Joplin	2	10
5/1/72	5/22/72	Me And Julio Down By The Schoolyard	Paul Simon	19	5
11/27/72	12/25/72	Me And Mrs. Jones	Billy Paul	1	12
3/22/71	4/26/71	Me And You And A Dog Named Boo	Lobo	3	9
4/26/71	5/10/71	Melting Pot	Booker T. & the MG's	27	3
7/5/71	8/9/71	Mercy Mercy Me (The Ecology)	Marvin Gaye	3	9
5/11/74	6/15/74	Midnight At The Oasis	Maria Muldaur	7	10
7/19/75	8/23/75	Midnight Blue	Melissa Manchester	5	14
11/17/69	1/12/70	Midnight Cowboy	Ferrante & Teicher	6	12
12/29/73	2/2/74	Midnight Rider	Gregg Allman	18	8
9/22/73	11/17/73	Midnight Train To Georgia	Gladys Knight & the Pips	6	14
7/19/71	8/2/71	Mighty Clouds Of Joy	B.J. Thomas	9	5
8/25/73	9/29/73	Million To One, A	Donny Osmond	20	7
11/10/73	12/15/73	Mind Games	John Lennon	6	13
6/16/79	7/14/79	Minute By Minute	Doobie Brothers	19	11
10/25/75	11/15/75	Miracles	Jefferson Starship	3	15
7/16/73	7/30/73	Misdemeanor	Foster Sylvers	26	3
2/25/78	4/8/78	Miss Broadway	Belle Epoque	27	14
6/24/78	8/19/78	Miss You	Rolling Stones	1	28
6/15/70	8/3/70	Mississippi Queen	Mountain	12	10
5/1/76	6/26/76	Misty Blue	Dorothy Moore	7	16
3/2/74	3/30/74	Mockingbird	Carly Simon & James Taylor	7	12
6/4/73	7/16/73	Money	Pink Floyd	10	9
2/21/76	3/20/76	Money Honey	Bay City Rollers	7	14
6/25/73	7/9/73	Monster Mash	Bobby "Boris" Pickett & the Crypt-Kickers	3	9
10/19/70	11/30/70	Montego Bay	Bobby Bloom	2	13
7/5/71	8/2/71	Moon Shadow	Cat Stevens	13	6
6/19/76	7/31/76	Moonlight Feels Right	Starbuck	21	12
5/15/76	7/31/76	More, More, More Pt. 1	Andrea True Connection	9	21
10/16/76	12/4/76	More Than A Feeling	Boston	2	18
8/2/75	8/16/75	Mornin' Beautiful	Tony Orlando & Dawn	19	3
7/9/73	8/11/73	Morning After, The	Maureen McGovern	2	13
5/1/72	5/29/72	Morning Has Broken	Cat Stevens	6	8
8/10/70	8/17/70	Morning Much Better	Ten Wheel Drive with Genya Ravan	21	3
12/28/74	2/1/75	Morning Side Of The Mountain	Donny & Marie Osmond	5	12

Debut	Peak	Title	Artist	Pos	Wks
12/1/73	2/2/74	Most Beautiful Girl, The	Charlie Rich	1	16
12/28/70	1/25/71	Most Of All	B.J. Thomas	18	6
2/28/72	3/27/72	Mother And Child Reunion	Paul Simon	2	10
8/9/71	8/16/71	Mother Freedom	Bread	21	3
7/31/72	8/21/72	Motorcycle Mama	Sailcat	12	8
5/29/76	6/19/76	Movin'	Brass Construction	26	6
6/14/71	7/12/71	Mr. Big Stuff	Jean Knight	4	8
2/8/71	3/1/71	Mr. Bojangles	Nitty Gritty Dirt Band	11	6
9/13/75	10/11/75	Mr. Jaws	Dickie Goodman	1	8
3/24/79	4/21/79	Music Box Dancer	Frank Mills	2	17
10/2/76	11/13/76	Muskrat Love	Captain & Tennille	1	22
8/12/78	9/9/78	My Angel Baby	Toby Beau	20	11
5/4/70	6/22/70	My Baby Loves Lovin'	White Plains	2	11
1/19/70	2/9/70	My Elusive Dreams	Bobby Vinton	15	7
2/15/75	3/22/75	My Eyes Adored You	Frankie Valli	2	15
6/1/74	6/15/74	My Girl Bill	Jim Stafford	8	4
7/2/77	8/27/77	My Heart Belongs To Me	Barbra Streisand	18	13
12/29/69	1/26/70	My Honey And Me	Luther Ingram	19	6
11/25/78	1/20/79	My Life	Billy Joel	3	22
12/6/75	1/10/76	My Little Town	Simon & Garfunkel	5	15
5/14/73	6/4/73	My Love	Paul McCartney	1	10
9/15/73	10/13/73	My Maria	B.W. Stevenson	13	8
10/26/74	11/30/74	My Melody Of Love	Bobby Vinton	2	15
7/28/79	8/18/79	My Sharona	Knack	1	27
11/23/70	12/7/70	My Sweet Lord	George Harrison	1	11
12/10/77	1/7/78	My Way	Elvis Presley	18	10
2/7/72	2/28/72	My World	Bee Gees	9	9
10/27/69	12/1/69	Na Na Hey Hey Kiss Him Goodbye	Steam	1	13
10/30/76	12/25/76	Nadia's Theme (The Young And The Restless)	Barry DeVorzon & Perry Botkin, Jr.	1	22
5/17/71	6/28/71	Nathan Jones	Supremes	3	9
1/21/78	3/4/78	Native New Yorker	Odyssey	18	13
6/11/73	7/2/73	Natural High	Bloodstone	11	7
11/15/71	12/6/71	Natural Man, A	Lou Rawls	16	6
8/10/70	9/7/70	Neanderthal Man	Hotlegs	4	9
2/26/73	4/2/73	Neither One Of Us	Gladys Knight & the Pips	4	9
1/10/72	2/14/72	Never Been To Spain	Three Dog Night	5	10
1/11/75	2/8/75	Never Can Say Goodbye	Gloria Gaynor	8	11
3/22/71	5/10/71	Never Can Say Goodbye	Jackson 5	2	12
7/5/71	8/2/71	Never Ending Song Of Love	Delaney & Bonnie & Friends	2	8
5/22/76	7/3/76	Never Gonna Fall In Love Again	Eric Carmen	7	14
2/2/70	3/9/70	Never Had A Dream Come True	Stevie Wonder	23	6
2/17/79	3/10/79	Never Had A Love	Tavares	28	8
8/26/78	9/23/78	Never Make A Move Too Soon	B.B. King	31	10
9/21/74	10/19/74	Never My Love	Blue Swede	8	6

Debut	Peak	Title	Artist	Pos	Wks
10/4/71	11/1/71	Never My Love	Fifth Dimension	10	8
12/8/73	2/16/74	Never, Never Gonna Give Ya Up	Barry White	10	13
12/25/76	2/19/77	New Kid In Town	Eagles	2	18
5/1/72	6/19/72	Nice To Be With You	Gallery	1	12
2/7/72	3/6/72	Nickel Song, The	Melanie	18	5
7/27/74	8/10/74	Night Chicago Died, The	Paper Lace	1	15
2/25/78	5/6/78	Night Fever	Bee Gees	1	26
1/15/77	3/12/77	Night Moves	Bob Seger	3	19
3/26/73	4/9/73	Night The Lights Went Out In Georgia, The	Vicki Lawrence	1	10
8/16/71	9/20/71	Night They Drove Old Dixie Down, The	Joan Baez	2	11
10/30/76	12/18/76	Nights Are Forever Without You	England Dan & John Ford Coley	7	14
9/18/72	10/30/72	Nights In White Satin	Moody Blues	1	11
11/15/75	12/6/75	Nights On Broadway	Bee Gees	7	15
1/4/71	1/25/71	1900 Yesterday	Liz Damon's Orient Express	10	7
3/29/71	4/12/71	No Love At All	B.J. Thomas	14	5
11/30/70	12/21/70	No Matter What	Badfinger	6	6
5/28/73	6/25/73	No More Mr. Nice Guy	Alice Cooper	16	6
11/3/79	12/1/79	No More Tears (Enough Is Enough)	Barbra Streisand/Donna Summer	2	18
3/8/75	5/3/75	No No Song	Ringo Starr	2	16
4/13/70	5/4/70	No Sugar Tonight	Guess Who	1	10
1/5/70	1/26/70	No Time	Guess Who	2	10
9/10/77	10/29/77	Nobody Does It Better	Carly Simon	3	18
9/14/74	10/12/74	Nothing From Nothing	Billy Preston	3	13
4/6/70	4/20/70	Nothing Succeeds Like Success	Bill Deal & the Rhondels	25	4
11/29/71	12/13/71	Nothing To Hide	Tommy James	11	7
11/27/76	12/11/76	Ob-La-Di, Ob-La-Da	Beatles	33	5
1/8/73	2/12/73	Oh, Babe, What Would You Say	Hurricane Smith	3	9
4/17/72	5/22/72	Oh Girl	Chi-Lites	1	13
3/31/79	4/21/79	Oh Honey	Delegation	27	10
2/2/70	3/2/70	Oh Me, Oh My (I'm A Fool For You Baby)	Lulu	19	5
3/30/74	4/13/74	Oh My My	Ringo Starr	16	6
6/8/74	6/8/74	Oh Very Young	Cat Stevens	19	1
5/17/75	6/28/75	Old Days	Chicago	10	11
11/22/71	12/13/71	Old Fashioned Love Song, An	Three Dog Night	3	9
8/13/77	10/29/77	On And On	Stephen Bishop	8	19
8/3/74	8/31/74	On And On	Gladys Knight & the Pips	13	5
4/29/78	6/10/78	On Broadway	George Benson	13	17
1/11/71	2/1/71	One Bad Apple	Osmonds	1	9
9/20/71	10/18/71	One Fine Morning	Lighthouse	10	7
11/16/70	12/14/70	One Less Bell To Answer	Fifth Dimension	2	11
11/30/70	12/14/70	One Man Band	Three Dog Night	15	5

Debut	Peak	Title	Artist	Pos	Wks
4/9/73	4/16/73	One Man Band (Plays All Alone)	Ronnie Dyson	18	3
12/14/74	12/28/74	One Man Woman/One Woman Man	Paul Anka with Odia Coates	10	6
12/6/71	1/10/72	One Monkey Don't Stop No Show Part I	Honey Cone	11	10
9/16/78	11/11/78	One Nation Under A Groove—Part I	Funkadelic	12	18
6/4/73	6/11/73	One Of A Kind (Love Affair)	Spinners	9	7
7/12/75	8/9/75	One Of These Nights	Eagles	7	13
2/9/70	2/16/70	One Tin Soldier	Original Caste	36	2
12/1/73	1/5/74	One Tin Soldier, The Legend Of Billy Jack	Coven	1	16
2/8/71	3/29/71	One Toke Over The Line	Brewer & Shipley	4	11
8/18/79	9/22/79	One Way Or Another	Blondie	31	15
2/21/76	4/3/76	Only Sixteen	Dr. Hook	7	15
7/15/78	8/12/78	Only The Good Die Young	Billy Joel	17	18
4/12/75	6/7/75	Only Yesterday	Carpenters	3	20
10/11/71	11/1/71	Only You Know And I Know	Delaney & Bonnie	7	8
10/6/73	11/24/73	Ooh Baby	Gilbert O'Sullivan	12	13
1/13/79	2/3/79	Ooh Baby Baby	Linda Ronstadt	14	11
6/15/70	7/20/70	O-o-h Child	Five Stairsteps	4	12
11/6/72	12/11/72	Operator (That's Not The Way It Feels)	Jim Croce	14	7
10/19/70	10/26/70	Our House	Crosby, Stills, Nash & Young	27	2
2/4/78	4/8/78	Our Love	Natalie Cole	11	18
9/7/70	10/4/70	Out In The Country	Three Dog Night	7	9
4/16/73	5/7/73	Out Of The Question	Gilbert O'Sullivan	19	4
5/15/72	7/3/72	Outa-Space	Billy Preston	2	11
12/27/75	2/28/76	Over My Head	Fleetwood Mac	11	18
7/16/73	7/23/73	Over The Hills And Far Away	Led Zeppelin	22	2
3/8/71	3/22/71	Oye Como Va	Santana	15	4
11/10/73	12/15/73	Painted Ladies	Ian Thomas	11	13
1/31/76	2/21/76	Paloma Blanca	George Baker Selection	32	10
11/13/72	12/4/72	Papa Was A Rollin' Stone	Temptations	1	9
9/29/73	11/17/73	Paper Roses	Marie Osmond	4	14
3/1/75	3/22/75	Part Of The Plan	Dan Fogelberg	18	4
12/23/78	1/13/79	Part-Time Love	Elton John	29	8
8/3/70	9/7/70	Patches	Clarence Carter	5	11
12/14/70	1/4/71	Pay To The Piper	Chairmen of the Board	13	6
5/21/77	7/9/77	Peace Of Mind	Boston	10	13
10/18/71	11/22/71	Peace Train	Cat Stevens	3	9
8/24/70	9/14/70	Peace Will Come (According To Plan)	Melanie	28	4
4/2/73	4/23/73	Peaceful	Helen Reddy	13	7
2/12/73	3/5/73	Peaceful Easy Feeling	Eagles	19	4
7/13/70	8/3/70	Pearl	Tommy Roe	25	4
1/28/78	2/18/78	Peg	Steely Dan	24	15

Debut	Peak	Title	Artist	Pos	Wks
4/27/70	5/11/70	People And Me	New Colony Six	32	4
7/17/72	7/24/72	People Make The World Go Round	Stylistics	21	2
3/8/75	4/12/75	Philadelphia Freedom	Elton John Band	1	23
10/6/73	11/24/73	Photograph	Ringo Starr	1	14
3/1/75	3/22/75	Pick Up The Pieces	Average White Band	12	5
12/11/72	1/15/73	Pieces Of April	Three Dog Night	17	6
4/23/73	6/11/73	Pillow Talk	Sylvia	2	10
4/19/75	5/10/75	Pinball Wizard	Elton John	16	24
4/23/73	4/23/73	Pinball Wizard/See Me, Feel Me	New Seekers	25	1
9/4/72	10/2/72	Play Me	Neil Diamond	10	7
8/7/76	9/25/76	Play That Funky Music	Wild Cherry	2	27
5/21/73	6/11/73	Playground In My Mind	Clint Holmes	8	15
8/24/74	9/7/74	Please Come To Boston	Dave Loggins	21	5
11/17/79	1/12/80	Please Don't Go	KC & The Sunshine Band	3	21
6/28/75	8/2/75	Please Mr. Please	Olivia Newton-John	4	14
12/14/74	1/18/75	Please Mr. Postman	Carpenters	1	17
3/22/75	4/5/75	Poetry Man	Phoebe Snow	15	3
12/3/77	1/28/78	Point Of Know Return	Kansas	11	14
9/29/79	12/22/79	Pop Muzik	M	3	23
9/4/72	9/18/72	Pop That Thang	Isley Brothers	21	4
8/21/72	9/25/72	Power Of Love	Joe Simon	11	7
4/5/71	5/3/71	Power To The People	John Lennon & the Plastic Ono Band	9	7
1/24/72	2/14/72	Precious And Few	Climax	2	9
3/9/74	3/9/74	Press My Conference	John Records Landecker	23	2
1/27/79	2/17/79	Promises	Eric Clapton	30	8
2/8/71	3/1/71	Proud Mary	Ike & Tina Turner	6	7
1/12/70	2/9/70	Psychedelic Shack	Temptations	4	11
4/20/70	5/18/70	Puppet Man	Fifth Dimension	14	7
5/10/71	6/7/71	Puppet Man	Tom Jones	22	5
3/13/72	3/27/72	Puppy Love	Donny Osmond	3	8
3/22/71	5/3/71	Put Your Hand In The Hand	Ocean	2	10
5/11/70	6/22/70	Question	Moody Blues	13	10
7/13/74	8/10/74	Radar Love	Golden Earring	4	10
9/27/71	10/11/71	Rain Dance	Guess Who	24	3
11/17/69	12/22/69	Raindrops Keep Fallin' On My Head	B.J. Thomas	2	13
5/3/71	6/14/71	Rainy Days And Mondays	Carpenters	2	11
6/21/71	7/12/71	Rainy Jane	Davy Jones	14	5
1/26/70	3/16/70	Rainy Night In Georgia	Brook Benton	4	12
9/29/73	10/27/73	Raised On Rock	Elvis Presley	30	6
9/8/73	10/13/73	Ramblin Man	Allman Brothers Band	3	13
1/26/70	3/2/70	Rapper, The	Jaggerz	2	12
11/10/79	12/22/79	Rapper's Delight	Sugarhill Gang	17	18
4/27/70	6/1/70	Reach Out And Touch (Somebody's Hand)	Diana Ross	15	9
4/19/71	5/17/71	Reach Out I'll Be There	Diana Ross	9	7

Debut	Peak	Title	Artist	Pos	Wks
4/1/78	4/22/78	Reachin' For The Sky	Peabo Bryson	41	3
10/14/78	12/2/78	Ready To Take A Chance Again	Barry Manilow	10	16
10/2/76	11/13/76	Reaper, (Don't Fear) The	Blue Oyster Cult	5	16
8/30/71	9/27/71	Reason To Believe	Rod Stewart	1	13
5/4/70	5/11/70	Red Red Wine	Vic Dana	36	3
4/16/73	5/28/73	Reeling In The Years	Steely Dan	7	8
3/23/70	5/11/70	Reflections Of My Life	Marmalade	2	14
12/28/70	2/1/71	Remember Me	Diana Ross	4	10
9/30/78	11/4/78	Reminiscing	Little River Band	6	16
4/28/79	6/2/79	Renegade	Styx	6	22
11/15/71	12/27/71	Respect Yourself	Staple Singers	3	12
7/19/71	8/30/71	Resurrection Shuffle	Ashton, Gardner & Dyke	5	11
3/31/79	5/19/79	Reunited	Peaches & Herb	1	21
4/3/76	5/8/76	Rhiannon (Will You Ever Win)	Fleetwood Mac	6	15
8/16/75	9/6/75	Rhinestone Cowboy	Glen Campbell	1	23
2/12/77	4/16/77	Rich Girl	Daryl Hall & John Oates	1	22
5/11/70	6/22/70	Ride Captain Ride	Blues Image	3	12
7/5/71	8/16/71	Riders On The Storm	Doors	1	11
3/20/76	5/1/76	Right Back Where We Started From	Maxine Nightingale	2	15
10/14/78	11/25/78	Right Down The Line	Gerry Rafferty	19	12
5/14/73	7/2/73	Right Place Wrong Time	Dr. John	5	10
4/30/73	5/28/73	Right Thing To Do, The	Carly Simon	12	5
3/19/77	5/28/77	Right Time Of The Night	Jennifer Warnes	8	18
6/29/74	7/13/74	Rikki Don't Lose That Number	Steely Dan	3	11
6/9/79	7/21/79	Ring My Bell	Anita Ward	1	18
2/14/72	3/6/72	Ring The Living Bell	Melanie	20	4
6/28/71	7/26/71	Rings	Cymarron	17	6
9/8/79	10/27/79	Rise	Herb Alpert	1	23
11/30/70	12/28/70	River Deep—Mountain High	Supremes & the Four Tops	11	8
8/14/72	9/18/72	Rock And Roll Part 2	Gary Glitter	5	8
12/27/75	1/31/76	Rock And Roll All Nite	Kiss	6	17
7/6/74	7/27/74	Rock And Roll Heaven	Righteous Brothers	10	5
3/16/74	3/16/74	Rock And Roll, Hoochie Koo	Rick Derringer	20	2
5/8/76	6/26/76	Rock And Roll Love Letter	Bay City Rollers	4	15
3/6/72	4/3/72	Rock And Roll Lullaby	B.J. Thomas	5	9
6/5/76	7/31/76	Rock And Roll Music	Beach Boys	2	19
8/24/74	9/21/74	Rock Me Gently	Andy Kim	1	13
11/17/73	11/24/73	Rock 'N Roll (I Gave You The Best Years Of My Life)	Kevin Johnson	37	2
6/2/79	8/4/79	Rock 'N' Roll Fantasy	Bad Company	9	19
11/20/72	11/20/72	Rock 'N Roll Soul	Grand Funk Railroad	26	1
2/9/74	3/16/74	Rock On	David Essex	1	11
11/1/71	11/15/71	Rock Steady	Aretha Franklin	16	4
6/15/74	7/6/74	Rock The Boat	Hues Corporation	1	14
12/29/79	2/9/80	Rock With You	Michael Jackson	1	24

Debut	Peak	Title	Artist	Pos	Wks
7/6/74	8/3/74	Rock Your Baby	George McCrae	1	11
6/12/72	7/10/72	Rocket Man	Elton John	8	8
8/16/75	8/30/75	Rockford Files, The	Mike Post	12	5
7/12/75	8/23/75	Rockin' Chair	Gwen McCrae	10	8
10/30/72	1/15/73	Rockin' Pneumonia— Boogie Woogie Flu	Johnny Rivers	5	15
3/20/72	4/24/72	Rockin' Robin	Michael Jackson	2	9
12/15/73	2/9/74	Rockin' Roll Baby	Stylistics	8	11
9/25/76	11/6/76	Rock'n Me	Steve Miller	3	18
10/18/75	11/15/75	Rocky	Austin Roberts	8	15
1/15/73	3/12/73	Rocky Mountain High	John Denver	6	10
10/6/73	11/3/73	Rocky Mountain Way	Joe Walsh	24	7
1/25/75	3/8/75	Roll On Down The Highway	Bachman-Turner Overdrive	4	15
8/11/73	9/1/73	Roll Over Beethoven	Electric Light Orchestra	8	8
1/4/71	1/18/71	Rose Garden	Lynn Anderson	23	3
3/13/72	4/10/72	Roundabout	Yes	7	9
9/29/73	11/3/73	Rubber Bullets	10cc	23	9
8/31/70	9/21/70	Rubber Duckie	Ernie (Jim Henson)	6	5
11/6/76	12/25/76	Rubberband Man, The	Spinners	4	18
8/23/75	9/20/75	Run Joey Run	David Geddes	2	13
4/17/72	5/8/72	Run Run Run	Jo Jo Gunne	10	6
8/28/72	9/18/72	Run To Me	Bee Gees	14	7
11/19/77	1/7/78	Runaround Sue	Leif Garrett	1	17
7/22/78	8/12/78	Runaway	Jefferson Starship	27	9
6/3/78	7/22/78	Runaway Love	Linda Clifford	19	15
3/6/72	3/20/72	Runnin' Away	Sly & the Family Stone	24	4
4/8/78	5/13/78	Running On Empty	Jackson Browne	14	14
7/24/72	7/24/72	Runway, The	Grass Roots	24	1
8/18/79	9/29/79	Sad Eyes	Robert John	2	24
9/15/79	11/3/79	Sail On	Commodores	5	20
3/12/77	4/16/77	Sam	Olivia Newton-John	30	7
5/8/76	7/10/76	Sara Smile	Daryl Hall & John Oates	9	21
8/21/72	9/25/72	Saturday In The Park	Chicago	3	9
11/29/75	12/20/75	Saturday Night	Bay City Rollers	1	25
8/11/73	9/22/73	Saturday Night's Alright For Fighting	Elton John	4	12
6/22/70	7/6/70	Save The Country	Fifth Dimension	17	5
1/19/70	2/9/70	Save The Country	Thelma Houston	18	5
7/23/73	9/22/73	Say, Has Anybody Seen My Sweet Gypsy Rose	Dawn featuring Tony Orlando	8	11
7/17/76	8/21/76	Say You Love Me	Fleetwood Mac	9	15
2/19/77	4/16/77	Say You'll Stay Until Tomorrow	Tom Jones	19	13
11/29/71	1/17/72	Scorpio	Dennis Coffey	4	13
7/17/72	8/7/72	Sealed With A Kiss	Bobby Vinton	18	4
5/4/74	5/25/74	(I've Been) Searchin' So Long	Chicago	12	5
1/12/74	2/9/74	Seasons In The Sun	Terry Jacks	1	20
12/27/75	12/27/75	Secret Love	Freddy Fender	36	2
11/2/70	11/30/70	See Me, Feel Me	Who	5	8

Debut	Peak	Title	Artist	Pos	Wks
5/4/70	5/11/70	Seeker, The	Who	33	3
11/5/77	12/17/77	Send In The Clowns	Judy Collins	13	12
12/1/79	1/19/80	Send One Your Love	Stevie Wonder	20	13
12/3/77	1/14/78	Sentimental Lady	Bob Welch	8	13
1/22/73	1/22/73	Separate Ways	Elvis Presley	21	2
12/16/78	2/10/79	September	Earth, Wind & Fire	3	22
5/6/78	6/10/78	Shadow Dancing	Andy Gibb	1	24
8/4/79	8/25/79	Shadows In The Moonlight	Anne Murray	34	8
10/11/71	11/8/71	Shaft, Theme From	Isaac Hayes	1	13
1/20/79	2/17/79	Shake It	Ian Matthews	17	13
4/7/79	5/26/79	Shake Your Body (Down To The Ground)	Jacksons	4	22
7/31/76	9/18/76	(Shake, Shake, Shake) Shake Your Booty	KC & the Sunshine Band	3	17
2/10/79	3/24/79	Shake Your Groove Thing	Peaches & Herb	4	24
11/20/76	11/27/76	Shake Your Rump To The Funk	Bar-Kays	42	4
12/7/74	12/21/74	Sha-La-La (Make Me Happy)	Al Green	12	4
6/4/73	7/23/73	Shambala	Three Dog Night	1	12
5/27/78	7/1/78	Shame	Evelyn "Champagne" King	17	27
4/10/76	6/5/76	Shannon	Henry Gross	2	18
10/26/70	12/7/70	Share The Land	Guess Who	3	10
12/2/78	1/20/79	Sharing The Night Together	Dr. Hook	14	16
3/22/75	4/26/75	Shaving Cream	Benny Bell	12	8
12/8/69	12/29/69	She	Tommy James & the Shondells	23	6
6/9/79	8/4/79	She Believes In Me	Kenny Rogers	7	27
1/5/70	1/19/70	She Belongs To Me	Rick Nelson	31	3
9/24/77	11/19/77	She Did It	Eric Carmen	6	17
1/25/71	4/5/71	She's A Lady	Tom Jones	1	14
9/4/76	10/23/76	She's Gone	Daryl Hall & John Oates	9	14
4/26/71	6/7/71	She's Not Just Another Woman	8th Day	8	8
12/17/77	1/7/78	She's Not There	Santana	37	5
3/16/70	4/13/70	Shilo	Neil Diamond	14	6
6/30/79	7/28/79	Shine A Little Love	Electric Light Orchestra	13	14
5/24/75	6/7/75	Shining Star	Earth, Wind & Fire	9	7
10/13/79	12/8/79	Ships	Barry Manilow	13	17
5/8/76	6/26/76	Shop Around	Captain & Tennille	1	18
12/24/77	1/28/78	Short People	Randy Newman	2	19
3/18/78	3/18/78	Shout It Out	B.T. Express	44	1
11/17/73	12/29/73	Show And Tell	Al Wilson	2	14
4/3/76	5/8/76	Show Me The Way	Peter Frampton	8	14
5/4/74	5/25/74	Show Must Go On, The	Three Dog Night	6	9
9/10/77	10/22/77	Signed, Sealed, Delivered (I'm Yours)	Peter Frampton	9	13
6/29/70	8/17/70	Signed, Sealed, Delivered I'm Yours	Stevie Wonder	2	13
7/12/71	8/23/71	Signs	Five Man Electrical Band	2	12
4/24/76	5/29/76	Silly Love Songs	Wings	1	22

Debut	Peak	Title	Artist	Pos	Wks
7/13/70	8/3/70	Silver Bird	Mark Lindsay	21	5
3/19/73	4/23/73	Sing	Carpenters	4	11
1/3/76	1/24/76	Sing A Song	Earth, Wind & Fire	14	12
4/9/77	6/4/77	Sir Duke	Stevie Wonder	1	18
5/10/75	6/21/75	Sister Golden Hair	America	1	18
12/1/73	1/19/74	Sister Mary Elephant (Shudd-Up!)	Cheech & Chong	3	13
12/11/72	1/8/73	Sitting	Cat Stevens	15	6
12/22/69	12/29/69	Six White Horses	Tommy Cash	37	3
10/26/74	11/9/74	Skin Tight	Ohio Players	13	3
11/22/75	12/13/75	Sky High	Jigsaw	4	17
8/6/77	8/20/77	Slide	Slave	36	5
12/24/77	2/4/78	Slip Slidin' Away	Paul Simon	13	11
5/1/72	5/15/72	Slippin' Into Darkness	War	19	4
6/11/77	7/16/77	Slow Dancin' Don't Turn Me On	Addrisi Brothers	31	8
3/6/76	4/10/76	Slow Ride	Foghat	8	15
9/20/71	10/11/71	Smackwater Jack	Carole King	10	6
7/26/71	8/23/71	Smiling Faces Sometimes	Undisputed Truth	1	10
8/6/77	9/17/77	Smoke From A Distant Fire	Sanford/Townsend Band	20	12
6/18/73	7/30/73	Smoke On The Water	Deep Purple	5	12
11/24/73	1/12/74	Smokin' In The Boy's Room	Brownsville Station	2	13
8/31/70	9/14/70	Snowbird	Anne Murray	20	6
9/6/71	10/11/71	So Far Away	Carole King	10	8
2/19/77	4/9/77	So In To You	Atlanta Rhythm Section	8	18
7/6/70	7/6/70	So Much Love	Faith, Hope & Charity	38	1
6/18/73	7/9/73	So Very Hard To Go	Tower of Power	17	6
4/22/78	5/13/78	Softly As I Leave You	Elvis Presley	35	7
8/24/70	9/7/70	Solitary Man	Neil Diamond	18	7
8/30/71	9/20/71	Solo	Billie Sans	22	4
2/8/75	3/8/75	Some Kind Of Wonderful	Grand Funk	6	12
1/1/77	1/29/77	Somebody To Love	Queen	18	10
10/4/70	11/2/70	Somebody's Been Sleeping	100 Proof Aged In Soul	6	9
1/4/71	1/4/71	Somebody's Watching You	Little Sister	31	1
6/5/72	6/12/72	Someday Never Comes	Creedence Clearwater Revival	25	2
11/10/69	12/8/69	Someday We'll Be Together	Diana Ross & the Supremes	1	14
7/26/75	8/23/75	Someone Saved My Life Tonight	Elton John	1	18
1/29/77	2/5/77	Someone To Lay Down Beside Me	Linda Ronstadt	38	3
10/6/69	11/3/69	Something	Beatles	1	16
6/26/76	7/24/76	Something He Can Feel	Aretha Franklin	26	10
3/16/70	4/27/70	Something's Burning	Kenny Rogers & the First Edition	4	11
11/20/72	12/25/72	Something's Wrong With Me	Austin Roberts	10	7

Debut	Peak	Title	Artist	Pos	Wks
1/7/78	3/11/78	Sometimes When We Touch	Dan Hill	6	20
2/3/79	3/3/79	Somewhere In The Night	Barry Manilow	20	9
2/28/72	3/27/72	Son Of My Father	Giorgio	23	6
6/8/70	7/13/70	Song Of Joy, A	Miguel Rios	9	10
5/8/72	6/26/72	Song Sung Blue	Neil Diamond	1	12
4/27/70	5/18/70	Soolaimon (African Trilogy II)	Neil Diamond	22	7
6/21/71	7/26/71	Sooner Or Later	Grass Roots	5	8
7/3/76	8/14/76	Sophisticated Lady (She's A Different Lady)	Natalie Cole	33	9
12/4/76	1/15/77	Sorry Seems To Be The Hardest Word	Elton John	12	13
10/25/75	11/22/75	SOS	ABBA	6	16
6/25/73	7/9/73	Soul Makossa	Manu Dibango	28	3
2/3/79	3/3/79	Soul Man	Blues Brothers	11	14
3/26/77	4/30/77	Southern Nights	Glen Campbell	1	18
4/2/73	4/2/73	Space Oddity	David Bowie	22	2
10/27/73	12/15/73	Space Race	Billy Preston	12	13
8/9/71	9/6/71	Spanish Harlem	Aretha Franklin	1	11
9/11/72	10/2/72	Speak To The Sky	Rick Springfield	16	5
3/2/74	4/13/74	Spiders & Snakes	Jim Stafford	4	13
7/13/70	8/17/70	Spill The Wine	Eric Burdon & War	1	12
2/23/70	3/23/70	Spirit In The Sky	Norman Greenbaum	1	12
11/3/79	11/24/79	Spooky	Atlanta Rhythm Section	32	7
1/10/76	3/13/76	Squeeze Box	Who	17	16
8/23/71	9/13/71	Stagger Lee	Tommy Roe	12	7
10/26/70	11/16/70	Stand By Your Man	Candi Staton	20	5
11/6/76	1/8/77	Stand Tall	Burton Cummings	3	19
5/11/74	5/25/74	Star Baby	Guess Who	3	12
1/22/77	3/19/77	Star Is Born, Love Theme From A, (Evergreen)	Barbra Streisand	1	21
5/5/79	6/2/79	Star Love	Cheryl Lynn	22	10
8/6/77	9/17/77	Star Wars (Main Title)	John Williams & the London Symphony Orchestra	11	20
9/10/77	10/22/77	Star Wars Theme/Cantina Band	Meco	2	22
10/2/72	10/16/72	Starting All Over Again	Mel & Tim	19	6
5/20/78	6/17/78	Stay	Rufus featuring Chaka Khan	26	10
4/5/71	4/26/71	Stay Awhile	Bells	6	8
1/3/72	2/7/72	Stay With Me	Faces	4	10
1/7/78	2/11/78	Stayin' Alive	Bee Gees	1	31
11/16/70	12/21/70	Stealer	Free	19	5
5/14/73	6/4/73	Steamroller Blues	Elvis Presley	16	6
6/26/76	7/10/76	Steppin' Out	Neil Sedaka	35	5
8/9/71	9/20/71	Stick-Up	Honey Cone	5	11
11/3/79	12/15/79	Still	Commodores	5	19
8/21/76	10/16/76	Still The One	Orleans	6	18
7/8/78	8/19/78	Still The Same	Bob Seger & the Silver Bullet Band	14	14
11/2/70	11/16/70	Still Water (Love)	Four Tops	19	4
3/19/73	4/23/73	Stir It Up	Johnny Nash	10	8

Debut	Peak	Title	Artist	Pos	Wks
2/23/70	3/23/70	Stir It Up And Serve It	Tommy Roe	21	6
11/9/70	12/28/70	Stoned Love	Supremes	3	12
11/8/71	12/13/71	Stones	Neil Diamond	9	9
12/21/70	1/11/71	Stoney End	Barbra Streisand	11	7
9/28/74	10/26/74	Stop And Smell The Roses	Mac Davis	8	6
8/30/71	9/13/71	Story In Your Eyes, The	Moody Blues	14	6
12/9/78	12/23/78	Straight On	Heart	28	9
4/24/76	5/29/76	Strange Magic	Electric Light Orchestra	33	8
12/16/78	1/13/79	Strange Way	Firefall	26	10
8/13/77	10/15/77	Strawberry Letter 23	Brothers Johnson	24	13
4/27/74	5/11/74	Streak, The	Ray Stevens	1	11
2/18/78	2/25/78	Street Corner Serenade	Wet Willie	42	2
4/9/73	5/21/73	Stuck In The Middle With You	Stealers Wheel	4	8
7/1/78	7/22/78	Stuff Like That	Quincy Jones	25	13
4/7/79	5/19/79	Stumblin' In	Suzi Quatro & Chris Norman	11	18
4/10/72	5/15/72	Suavecito	Malo	5	9
12/13/71	1/24/72	Sugar Daddy	Jackson 5	4	12
6/8/70	7/13/70	Sugar, Sugar	Wilson Pickett	19	6
3/17/79	4/14/79	Sultans Of Swing	Dire Straits	9	14
7/31/76	9/11/76	Summer	War	10	14
10/13/73	11/10/73	Summer (The First Time)	Bobby Goldsboro	32	6
11/6/72	12/4/72	Summer Breeze	Seals & Crofts	5	8
8/26/78	10/21/78	Summer Nights	John Travolta & Olivia Newton-John	10	16
11/22/71	12/13/71	Summer Of '42, Theme From	Peter Nero	20	5
6/21/71	7/26/71	Summer Sand	Dawn	10	7
7/20/70	8/3/70	Summertime Blues	Who	16	6
5/25/74	6/22/74	Sundown	Gordon Lightfoot	1	14
8/13/77	9/3/77	Sunflower	Glen Campbell	38	5
11/20/72	12/4/72	Sunny Days	Lighthouse	26	3
9/11/76	10/9/76	Sunrise	Eric Carmen	35	8
7/20/70	8/3/70	Sunshine	Archies	26	3
11/29/71	12/27/71	Sunshine	Jonathan Edwards	2	13
2/16/74	3/9/74	Sunshine On My Shoulders	John Denver	4	11
12/11/72	1/22/73	Superfly	Curtis Mayfield	7	10
9/13/71	10/4/71	Superstar	Carpenters	3	10
4/26/71	5/10/71	Superstar	Murray Head With the Trinidad Singers	7	6
11/22/71	12/13/71	Superstar (Remember How You Got Where You Are)	Temptations	13	6
12/11/72	1/29/73	Superstition	Stevie Wonder	1	12
8/17/74	8/17/74	Sure As I'm Sittin' Here	Three Dog Night	17	1
10/22/77	11/5/77	Surfin' USA	Leif Garrett	30	6
8/26/78	9/16/78	Surrender	Cheap Trick	24	13
1/31/76	2/28/76	S.W.A.T., Theme From	Rhythm Heritage	3	20
8/20/77	10/29/77	Swayin' To The Music (Slow Dancin')	Johnny Rivers	7	18

Debut	Peak	Title	Artist	Pos	Wks
8/9/75	8/9/75	Swearin' To God	Frankie Valli	15	1
4/12/71	5/24/71	Sweet And Innocent	Donny Osmond	2	10
9/1/73	9/29/73	Sweet Charlie Babe	Jackie Moore	8	8
8/30/71	10/4/71	Sweet City Woman	Stampeders	2	11
7/12/71	8/16/71	Sweet Hitch-Hiker	Creedence Clearwater Revival	3	9
9/21/74	10/19/74	Sweet Home Alabama	Lynyrd Skynyrd	3	13
3/20/76	5/8/76	Sweet Love	Commodores	17	12
1/25/71	2/22/71	Sweet Mary	Wadsworth Mansion	5	8
1/10/72	2/28/72	Sweet Seasons	Carole King	8	14
11/27/72	12/25/72	Sweet Surrender	Bread	14	5
2/1/75	2/15/75	Sweet Surrender	John Denver	13	4
4/15/78	5/27/78	Sweet Talkin' Woman	Electric Light Orchestra	21	14
2/14/76	4/3/76	Sweet Thing	Rufus featuring Chaka Khan	14	14
11/19/77	12/10/77	Swingtown	Steve Miller Band	28	8
4/24/72	6/5/72	Sylvia's Mother	Dr. Hook & the Medicine Show	2	12
6/17/78	8/5/78	Take A Chance On Me	ABBA	7	17
2/16/70	3/16/70	Take A Look Around	Smith	19	6
6/19/72	7/17/72	Take It Easy	Eagles	9	7
1/17/76	2/28/76	Take It To The Limit	Eagles	24	13
8/2/71	9/13/71	Take Me Girl, I'm Ready	Jr. Walker & The All Stars	7	9
4/14/79	6/2/79	Take Me Home	Cher	8	16
6/28/71	8/16/71	Take Me Home, Country Roads	John Denver	2	12
9/30/78	10/28/78	Take Me I'm Yours	Michael Henderson	35	6
5/31/75	7/12/75	Take Me In Your Arms (Rock Me)	Doobie Brothers	8	14
5/13/78	6/10/78	Take Me To The Next Phase	Isley Brothers	27	13
2/24/79	3/17/79	Take That To The Bank	Shalamar	39	5
11/17/79	12/29/79	Take The Long Way Home	Supertramp	10	14
5/29/76	7/24/76	Take The Money And Run	Steve Miller	15	14
7/13/74	8/17/74	Takin' Care Of Business	Bachman-Turner Overdrive	2	12
5/22/76	6/26/76	Takin' It To The Streets	Doobie Brothers	15	11
5/17/71	6/7/71	Tarkio Road	Brewer & Shipley	12	5
3/27/72	4/24/72	Taurus	Dennis Coffey	16	6
6/1/70	7/6/70	Teach Your Children	Crosby, Stills, Nash & Young	14	7
6/19/76	7/17/76	Tear The Roof Off The Sucker (Give Up The Funk)	Parliament	25	8
10/26/70	11/23/70	Tears Of A Clown, The	Smokey Robinson & The Miracles	1	11
7/10/76	8/7/76	Teddy Bear	Red Sovine	15	10
5/21/73	5/21/73	Teddy Bear Song	Barbara Fairchild	24	2
12/22/73	2/16/74	Teenage Lament '74	Alice Cooper	13	11
7/23/77	9/17/77	Telephone Line	Electric Light Orchestra	15	14
8/20/77	9/3/77	Telephone Man	Meri Wilson	35	4
12/8/73	1/5/74	Tell Her She's Lovely	El Chicano	21	8
8/10/74	8/31/74	Tell Me Something Good	Rufus	2	12

Debut	Peak	Title	Artist	Pos	Wks
3/2/70	3/9/70	Temma Harbour	Mary Hopkin	36	3
2/15/71	2/22/71	Temptation Eyes	Grass Roots	23	4
3/16/70	4/13/70	Tennessee Bird Walk	Jack Blanchard & Misty Morgan	12	8
5/17/75	6/28/75	Thank God I'm A Country Boy	John Denver	6	14
1/5/70	1/26/70	Thank You (Falettinme Be Mice Elf Agin)	Sly & the Family Stone	1	12
5/6/78	5/27/78	Thank You For Being A Friend	Andrew Gold	30	10
9/8/73	10/13/73	That Lady (Part 1)	Isley Brothers	14	11
9/18/76	10/23/76	That'll Be The Day	Linda Ronstadt	17	10
8/13/77	10/1/77	That's Rock 'N' Roll	Shaun Cassidy	1	26
11/15/75	12/6/75	That's The Way (I Like It)	KC & the Sunshine Band	1	24
5/10/71	6/14/71	That's The Way I've Always Heard It Should Be	Carly Simon	3	8
9/7/70	10/12/70	That's Where I Went Wrong	Poppy Family	8	9
8/31/74	10/12/74	Then Came You	Dionne Warwick & Spinners	6	13
4/10/76	5/8/76	There's A Kind Of A Hush (All Over The World)	Carpenters	25	8
7/2/73	7/9/73	There's No Me Without You	Manhattans	24	2
10/18/75	11/8/75	They Just Can't Stop It The (Games People Play)	Spinners	3	13
1/21/78	3/4/78	(Love Is) Thicker Than Water	Andy Gibb	2	23
2/5/77	3/26/77	Things We Do For Love	10cc	1	22
4/30/73	5/28/73	Thinking Of You	Loggins & Messina	15	6
10/4/75	10/11/75	Third Rate Romance	Amazing Rhythm Aces	12	3
7/17/76	8/28/76	This Masquerade	George Benson	15	12
9/18/76	11/6/76	This One's For You	Barry Manilow	7	18
11/27/76	1/15/77	This Song	George Harrison	7	14
12/27/75	12/27/75	This Will Be	Natalie Cole	40	2
7/15/78	9/2/78	Three Times A Lady	Commodores	1	23
1/26/70	2/16/70	Thrill Is Gone, The	B.B. King	30	4
10/9/72	11/20/72	Thunder And Lightning	Chi Coltrane	12	7
10/29/77	11/12/77	Thunder In My Heart	Leo Sayer	33	4
1/21/78	4/15/78	Thunder Island	Jay Ferguson	14	19
2/23/70	3/2/70	Ticket To Ride	Carpenters	35	2
3/26/73	4/30/73	Tie A Yellow Ribbon Round The Ole Oak Tree	Dawn featuring Tony Orlando	1	10
10/2/72	10/16/72	Tight Rope	Leon Russell	8	6
6/22/70	8/3/70	Tighter, Tighter	Alive and Kicking	3	12
12/1/73	1/12/74	Time In A Bottle	Jim Croce	3	12
11/18/78	12/23/78	Time Passages	Al Stewart	16	15
1/3/76	2/21/76	Times Of Your Life	Paul Anka	35	9
10/26/74	12/7/74	Tin Man	America	4	14
9/13/71	11/8/71	Tired Of Being Alone	Al Green	3	12

Debut	Peak	Title	Artist	Pos	Wks
6/5/76	7/24/76	Today's The Day	America	25	11
8/17/70	8/31/70	Tommy, Overture From	Assembled Multitude	19	4
2/15/71	2/15/71	Tongue In Cheek	Sugarloaf	31	1
10/21/78	11/18/78	Tonight's The Night	Betty Wright	29	7
10/23/76	11/20/76	Tonight's The Night (Gonna Be Alright)	Rod Stewart	1	21
6/5/72	7/17/72	Too Late To Turn Back Now	Cornelius Brothers & Sister Rose	2	12
12/2/78	2/3/79	Too Much Heaven	Bee Gees	3	23
4/1/78	5/27/78	Too Much, Too Little, Too Late	Johnny Mathis & Deniece Williams	1	22
7/3/72	7/17/72	Too Young	Donny Osmond	8	4
10/13/73	12/22/73	Top Of The World	Carpenters	2	19
8/25/79	9/22/79	Topical Song, The	Barron Knights	29	9
12/25/76	2/26/77	Torn Between Two Lovers	Mary MacGregor	1	23
7/2/73	7/30/73	Touch Me In The Morning	Diana Ross	1	13
1/5/70	1/19/70	Traces/Memories Medley	Lettermen	33	5
2/17/79	4/7/79	Tragedy	Bee Gees	4	20
6/22/74	7/6/74	Train Of Thought	Cher	10	4
10/18/71	11/8/71	Trapped By A Thing Called Love	Denise LaSalle	12	6
1/19/70	2/16/70	Travelin' Band	Creedence Clearwater Revival	3	6
4/12/71	5/31/71	Treat Her Like A Lady	Cornelius Brothers & Sister Rose	4	10
5/22/72	6/19/72	Troglodyte (Cave Man)	Jimmy Castor Bunch	5	5
1/8/73	2/5/73	Trouble Man	Marvin Gaye	9	7
4/10/76	5/22/76	Tryin' To Get The Feeling Again	Barry Manilow	8	13
3/26/77	4/30/77	Tryin' To Love Two	William Bell	25	9
4/6/74	5/11/74	TSOP (The Sound Of Philadelphia)	MFSB featuring the Three Degrees	5	12
3/30/74	4/20/74	Tubular Bells	Mike Oldfield	5	12
5/1/72	6/12/72	Tumbling Dice	Rolling Stones	4	10
3/23/70	4/27/70	Turn Back The Hands Of Time	Tyrone Davis	10	11
7/31/76	8/21/76	Turn The Beat Around	Vicki Sue Robinson	25	8
12/17/77	2/4/78	Turn To Stone	Electric Light Orchestra	11	18
8/30/75	9/13/75	Tush	ZZ Top	5	12
9/29/79	11/10/79	Tusk	Fleetwood Mac	6	20
4/9/73	5/21/73	Twelfth Of Never, The	Donny Osmond	6	8
8/3/70	8/31/70	25 Or 6 To 4	Chicago	2	9
10/25/71	11/22/71	Two Divided By Love	Grass Roots	9	7
7/22/78	9/2/78	Two Out Of Three Ain't Bad	Meat Loaf	11	19
8/2/71	8/23/71	Uncle Albert/Admiral Halsey	Paul & Linda McCartney	3	11
5/28/77	7/16/77	Undercover Angel	Alan O'Day	1	23
7/2/73	8/18/73	Uneasy Rider	Charlie Daniels	8	8
5/11/70	6/29/70	United We Stand	Brotherhood Of Man	15	10

Debut	Peak	Title	Artist	Pos	Wks
2/23/70	3/2/70	Until It's Time For You To Go	Neil Diamond	34	3
2/16/74	3/2/74	Until You Come Back To Me (That's What I'm Gonna Do)	Aretha Franklin	15	3
4/13/70	5/25/70	Up Around The Bend	Creedence Clearwater Revival	1	13
2/22/75	3/22/75	Up In A Puff Of Smoke	Polly Brown	9	5
11/10/69	12/15/69	Up On Cripple Creek	Band	11	10
3/9/70	4/20/70	Up The Ladder To The Roof	Supremes	3	12
9/18/72	10/23/72	Use Me	Bill Withers	2	8
5/13/78	7/8/78	Use Ta Be My Girl	O'Jays	8	20
3/23/70	4/27/70	Vehicle	Ides Of March	1	12
10/30/72	12/11/72	Ventura Highway	America	6	11
12/1/69	1/5/70	Venus	Shocking Blue	1	12
12/27/75	12/27/75	Venus And Mars Rock Show	Wings	23	4
4/20/70	5/18/70	Viva Tirado—Part I	El Chicano	19	9
12/22/69	1/26/70	Walk A Mile In My Shoes	Joe South	12	9
12/27/75	1/24/76	Walk Away From Love	David Ruffin	10	11
12/22/73	2/2/74	Walk Like A Man	Grand Funk	22	9
6/4/73	6/11/73	Walk On The Wild Side	Lou Reed	19	2
12/4/72	1/8/73	Walk On Water	Neil Diamond	20	5
12/18/76	1/29/77	Walk This Way	Aerosmith	4	15
12/22/69	2/2/70	Walkin' In The Rain	Jay & the Americans	11	9
5/22/72	6/12/72	Walkin' In The Rain With The One I Love	Love Unlimited	10	7
3/2/70	3/16/70	Walking Through The Country	Grass Roots	35	3
4/19/71	6/14/71	Want Ads	Honey Cone	1	12
8/3/70	8/24/70	War	Edwin Starr	1	12
1/11/71	2/8/71	Watching Scotty Grow	Bobby Goldsboro	4	9
6/28/71	7/19/71	Watching The River Flow	Bob Dylan	16	5
6/29/74	7/27/74	Waterloo	ABBA	3	11
12/17/77	1/28/78	Way I Feel Tonight, The	Bay City Rollers	19	11
11/8/75	12/6/75	Way I Want To Touch You, The	Captain & Tennille	2	15
2/14/72	3/13/72	Way Of Love, The	Cher	3	11
12/29/73	2/16/74	Way We Were, The	Barbra Streisand	2	15
3/18/78	4/1/78	Way You Do The Things You Do, The	Rita Coolidge	38	6
5/26/79	7/7/79	We Are Family	Sister Sledge	5	17
12/10/77	1/14/78	We Are The Champions	Queen	1	23
9/14/70	10/4/70	We Can Make Music	Tommy Roe	16	6
3/15/71	4/5/71	We Can Work It Out	Stevie Wonder	10	5
12/8/79	2/9/80	We Don't Talk Anymore	Cliff Richard	4	17
1/11/71	2/8/71	We Gotta Get You A Woman	Runt	11	7
10/29/77	12/10/77	We Just Disagree	Dave Mason	25	9

Debut	Peak	Title	Artist	Pos	Wks
9/22/73	11/17/73	We May Never Pass The Way (Again)	Seals & Crofts	8	13
12/24/77	1/14/78	We Will Rock You	Queen	1	21
7/30/73	9/22/73	We're An American Band	Grand Funk	1	13
8/9/71	9/6/71	Wedding Song (There Is Love)	Paul Stookey	2	10
12/11/76	1/29/77	Weekend In New England	Barry Manilow	1	21
4/17/76	5/8/76	Welcome Back	John Sebastian	1	14
4/15/78	5/13/78	We'll Never Have To Say Goodbye Again	England Dan & John Ford Coley	28	9
10/8/77	12/3/77	We're All Alone	Rita Coolidge	5	17
6/19/72	6/26/72	We're On Our Way	Chris Hodge	17	3
6/3/78	6/17/78	Werewolves Of London	Warren Zevon	32	8
7/13/70	7/27/70	Westbound #9	Flaming Ember	21	4
1/13/79	2/17/79	We've Got Tonite	Bob Seger & the Silver Bullet Band	19	12
9/28/70	10/26/70	We've Only Just Begun	Carpenters	2	11
8/14/76	10/23/76	Wham Bam	Silver	8	18
3/3/79	4/14/79	What A Fool Believes	Doobie Brothers	2	25
9/27/71	10/25/71	What Are You Doing Sunday	Dawn featuring Tony Orlando	10	8
3/1/71	3/29/71	What Is Life	George Harrison	5	8
4/13/70	5/11/70	What Is Truth	Johnny Cash	16	7
7/19/71	8/9/71	What The World Needs Now Is Love/Abraham, Martin And John	Tom Clay	4	5
1/27/79	3/3/79	What You Won't Do For Love	Bobby Caldwell	26	15
7/2/77	8/27/77	Whatcha Gonna Do	Pablo Cruise	6	15
8/16/71	8/30/71	Whatcha See Is Whatcha Get	Dramatics	10	6
10/19/74	11/23/74	Whatever Gets You Thru The Night	John Lennon	8	13
2/22/71	3/22/71	What's Going On	Marvin Gaye	3	9
1/14/78	2/25/78	What's Your Name	Lynyrd Skynyrd	15	15
3/19/77	5/14/77	When I Need You	Leo Sayer	1	21
1/11/71	2/1/71	When I'm Dead And Gone	McGuinness Flint	20	5
5/31/75	6/28/75	When Will I Be Loved	Linda Ronstadt	4	14
11/23/74	12/28/74	When Will I See You Again	Three Degrees	1	16
5/31/71	6/28/71	When You're Hot, You're Hot	Jerry Reed	10	6
7/28/79	9/1/79	When You're In Love With A Beautiful Woman	Dr. Hook	7	16
10/7/78	12/2/78	Whenever I Call You "Friend"	Kenny Loggins	8	17
12/6/71	12/27/71	Where Did Our Love Go	Donnie Elbert	7	8
3/29/71	3/29/71	Where Did They Go, Lord	Elvis Presley	31	1
6/26/72	8/14/72	Where Is The Love	Roberta Flack & Donny Hathaway	4	10
2/11/78	3/25/78	Which Way Is Up, Theme Song From	Stargard	18	13

Debut	Peak	Title	Artist	Pos	Wks
3/23/70	5/11/70	Which Way You Goin' Billy	Poppy Family	5	15
11/20/76	12/25/76	Whispering/Cherchez La Femme/Se Si Bon	Dr. Buzzard's Original "Savannah" Band	22	9
1/24/76	2/21/76	White Knight, The	Cledus Maggard & the Citizen's Band	20	12
12/27/71	1/17/72	White Lies, Blue Eyes	Bullet	5	9
10/7/78	11/11/78	Who Are You	Who	13	15
8/31/74	9/28/74	Who Do You Think You Are	Bo Donaldson & the Heywoods	5	13
11/1/75	11/29/75	Who Loves You	Four Seasons	2	15
11/24/69	1/5/70	Whole Lotta Love	Led Zeppelin	2	11
1/19/70	2/16/70	Who'll Stop The Rain	Creedence Clearwater Revival	3	12
12/8/73	12/22/73	Who's In The Strawberry Patch With Sally	Tony Orlando & Dawn	30	5
3/2/70	4/6/70	Who's Your Baby	Archies	22	6
9/11/72	10/9/72	Why	Donny Osmond	16	7
7/6/70	8/10/70	Why Can't I Touch You	Ronnie Dyson	3	10
7/19/75	8/16/75	Why Can't We Be Friends	War	6	14
12/25/72	1/29/73	Why Can't We Live Together	Timmy Thomas	5	10
12/15/79	2/2/80	Why Me	Styx	21	16
2/9/70	2/23/70	Why Should I Cry	Gentrys	31	3
11/8/71	11/29/71	Wild Night	Van Morrison	6	7
7/20/74	8/24/74	Wild Thing	Fancy	6	10
3/29/71	4/19/71	Wild World	Cat Stevens	19	5
6/7/75	6/28/75	Wildfire	Michael Murphey	1	16
4/16/73	5/28/73	Wildflower	Skylark	6	9
6/4/73	7/9/73	Will It Go Round In Circles	Billy Preston	1	10
12/13/75	12/27/75	Winners And Losers	Hamilton, Joe Frank & Reynolds	11	11
12/15/69	1/26/70	Winter World Of Love	Engelbert Humperdinck	13	9
11/23/74	12/7/74	Wishing You Were Here	Chicago	11	4
10/23/72	11/13/72	Witchy Woman	Eagles	9	7
4/22/78	6/17/78	With A Little Luck	Wings	4	19
8/14/76	9/25/76	With Your Love	Jefferson Starship	8	13
12/22/69	2/2/70	Without Love (There Is Nothing)	Tom Jones	7	10
1/24/72	2/28/72	Without You	Nilsson	1	13
3/27/76	5/1/76	Without Your Love (Mr. Jordan)	Charlie Ross	28	8
5/25/70	7/6/70	Wonder Of You, The	Elvis Presley	9	9
1/13/79	1/13/79	Wonder Worm	Captain Sky	44	1
3/25/78	4/22/78	(What A) Wonderful World	Art Garfunkel with James Taylor & Paul Simon	36	5
11/24/69	1/5/70	Wonderful World, Beautiful People	Jimmy Cliff	10	10
7/26/71	8/16/71	Won't Get Fooled Again	Who	15	5
3/16/70	5/11/70	Woodstock	Crosby, Stills, Nash & Young	4	12
1/15/73	2/5/73	World Is A Ghetto, The	War	10	6
9/11/76	10/30/76	Wreck Of The Edmund Fitzgerald, The	Gordon Lightfoot	3	20

Debut	Peak	Title	Artist	Pos	Wks
1/29/77	3/12/77	Year Of The Cat	Al Stewart	2	17
9/22/73	11/3/73	Yes We Can Can	Pointer Sisters	14	11
6/18/73	7/23/73	Yesterday Once More	Carpenters	4	12
1/1/77	1/29/77	Yesterday's Hero	Bay City Rollers	20	8
11/3/69	12/15/69	Yester-Me, Yester-You, Yesterday	Stevie Wonder	4	11
12/2/78	1/20/79	Y.M.C.A.	Village People	2	35
8/12/78	9/9/78	You	Rita Coolidge	21	12
10/19/74	11/16/74	You Ain't Seen Nothing Yet	Bachman-Turner Overdrive	1	16
8/5/78	9/30/78	You And I	Rick James	13	18
7/9/77	9/17/77	You And Me	Alice Cooper	10	16
12/6/71	1/10/72	You Are Everything	Stylistics	12	10
9/25/76	11/13/76	You Are My Starship	Norman Connors	23	12
3/15/75	4/12/75	You Are So Beautiful	Joe Cocker	7	13
4/2/73	5/21/73	You Are The Sunshine Of My Life	Stevie Wonder	1	9
10/16/76	12/11/76	You Are The Woman	Firefall	2	16
6/17/78	8/5/78	You Belong To Me	Carly Simon	11	17
5/21/73	5/21/73	You Can't Always Get What You Want	Rolling Stones	25	2
7/14/79	9/8/79	You Can't Change That	Raydio	10	16
12/31/77	1/28/78	You Can't Turn Me Off (In The Middle Of Turning Me On)	High Inergy	33	8
4/24/72	5/22/72	You Could Have Been A Lady	April Wine	14	7
10/20/79	11/17/79	You Decorated My Life	Kenny Rogers	14	16
11/11/78	12/23/78	You Don't Bring Me Flowers	Barbra & Neil	1	20
11/13/76	12/25/76	You Don't Have To Be A Star (To Be In My Show)	Marilyn McCoo & Billy Davis, Jr.	6	18
11/2/70	11/30/70	You Don't Have To Say You Love Me	Elvis Presley	7	7
7/24/72	9/4/72	You Don't Mess Around With Jim	Jim Croce	6	11
9/22/73	10/20/73	You Got Me Anyway	Sutherland Brothers & Quiver	10	9
12/21/74	1/4/75	You Got The Love	Rufus featuring Chaka Khan	14	5
10/2/76	10/30/76	You Gotta Make Your Own Sunshine	Neil Sedaka	31	6
10/5/74	10/5/74	You Haven't Done Nothin	Stevie Wonder	14	1
9/17/77	10/8/77	You Light Up My Life	Debby Boone	1	35
6/18/77	7/30/77	You Made Me Believe In Magic	Bay City Rollers	2	17
10/29/77	12/17/77	You Make Loving Fun	Fleetwood Mac	10	14
5/25/74	6/1/74	You Make Me Feel Brand New	Stylistics	12	6
11/6/76	12/18/76	You Make Me Feel Like Dancing	Leo Sayer	2	21
4/6/70	4/13/70	You Need Love Like I Do (Don't You)	Gladys Knight & The Pips	31	4

Debut	Peak	Title	Artist	Pos	Wks
9/23/78	11/25/78	You Needed Me	Anne Murray	4	25
10/28/78	12/2/78	You Never Done It Like That	Captain & Tennille	21	10
11/6/72	12/11/72	You Ought To Be With Me	Al Green	3	11
12/27/75	12/27/75	You Sexy Thing	Hot Chocolate	22	11
7/24/76	9/4/76	You Should Be Dancing	Bee Gees	5	17
6/9/79	7/7/79	You Take My Breath Away	Rex Smith	7	16
10/11/71	11/1/71	You Think You're Hot Stuff	Jean Knight	19	4
1/29/73	2/5/73	You Turn Me On, I'm A Radio	Joni Mitchell	19	2
9/18/72	10/16/72	You Wear It Well	Rod Stewart	11	7
6/22/74	7/20/74	You Won't See Me	Anne Murray	5	10
6/26/76	8/28/76	You'll Never Find Another Love Like Mine	Lou Rawls	4	18
6/25/73	7/2/73	You'll Never Get To Heaven (If You Break My Heart)	Stylistics	27	2
6/19/76	7/24/76	Young Hearts Run Free	Candi Staton	17	11
8/25/73	9/29/73	Young Love	Donny Osmond	20	7
4/23/77	5/14/77	Your Love	Marilyn McCoo & Billy Davis, Jr.	27	6
12/4/72	1/29/73	Your Mama Don't Dance	Loggins & Messina	4	12
11/26/77	12/24/77	Your Smiling Face	James Taylor	24	9
12/28/70	1/25/71	Your Song	Elton John	2	10
10/13/73	11/10/73	You're A Special Part Of Me	Diana Ross & Marvin Gaye	25	7
3/15/71	3/29/71	You're All I Need To Get By	Aretha Franklin	20	3
11/26/77	1/28/78	You're In My Heart (The Final Acclaim)	Rod Stewart	3	21
6/12/76	8/7/76	You're My Best Friend	Queen	4	16
7/9/77	9/3/77	You're My World	Helen Reddy	4	17
1/25/75	3/8/75	You're No Good	Linda Ronstadt	3	15
12/1/79	12/29/79	You're Only Lonely	J.D. Souther	12	14
12/15/73	2/9/74	You're Sixteen	Ringo Starr	2	16
12/11/72	1/8/73	You're So Vain	Carly Simon	1	14
12/21/74	1/4/75	You're The First, The Last, My Everything	Barry White	10	5
3/30/70	4/13/70	You're The One-Part I	Little Sister	34	3
4/29/78	6/17/78	You're The One That I Want	John Travolta & Olivia Newton-John	2	30
6/14/71	7/5/71	You've Got A Friend	James Taylor	2	9
9/20/71	10/25/71	Yo-Yo	Osmonds	1	11

Yearly Top 40 Charts

Top Hits of 1970:

1. Bridge Over Troubled Water   Simon & Garfunkel
2. Knock Three Times   Dawn
3. I'll Be There   Jackson 5
4. Make It With You   Bread
5. The Love You Save   Jackson 5
6. Thank You (Falettinme Be Mice Elf Agin)

    Sly & the Family Stone
7. Venus   Shocking Blue
8. War   Edwin Starr
9. I Think I Love You   Partridge Family
10. My Sweet Lord   George Harrison
11. Hitching A Ride   Vanity Fare
12. Cecilia   Simon & Garfunkel
13. Looking Out My Back Door   Creedence Clearwater Revival
14. ABC   Jackson 5
15. Tears Of A Clown   Smokey Robinson & the Miracles
16. Let It Be   Beatles
17. American Woman/No Sugar Tonight   Guess Who
18. Long & Winding Road   Beatles
19. Love Grows (Where My Rosemary Goes)   Edison Lighthouse
20. (They Long To Be) Close To You   Carpenters
21. Up Around The Bend   Creedence Clearwater Revival
22. Spirit In The Sky   Norman Greenbaum
23. Spill The Wine   Eric Burdon & War
24. Candida   Dawn

25.	Vehicle	Ides Of March
26.	Cracklin' Rosie	Neil Diamond
27.	Get Ready	Rare Earth
28.	No Time	Guess Who
29.	Montego Bay	Bobby Bloom
30.	Mama Told Me (Not To Come)	Three Dog Night
31.	The Rapper	Jaggerz
32.	Whole Lotta Love	Led Zeppelin
33.	Instant Karma (We All Shine On)	John Lennon
34.	Fire & Rain	James Taylor
35.	Gypsy Woman	Brian Hyland
36.	All Right Now	Free
37.	Reflections Of My Life	Marmalade
38.	Band Of Gold	Freda Payne
39.	Signed, Sealed, Delivered I'm Yours	Stevie Wonder
40.	I Just Can't Help Believing	B.J. Thomas

Top Hits of 1971:

1.	Joy To The World	Three Dog Night
2.	It's Too Late/I Feel The Earth Move	Carole King
3.	Maggie May/Reason To Believe	Rod Stewart
4.	Theme From Shaft	Isaac Hayes
5.	Mama's Pearl	Jackson 5
6.	She's A Lady	Tom Jones
7.	Go Away Little Girl	Donny Osmond
8.	Brand New Key	Melanie
9.	I Hear You Knocking	Dave Edmunds
10.	Doesn't Somebody Want To Be Wanted	Partridge Family
11.	Yo-Yo	Osmonds
12.	Brown Sugar	Rolling Stones
13.	Just My Imagination (Running Away With Me)	Temptations
14.	How Can You Mend A Broken Heart	Bee Gees
15.	Smiling Faces Sometimes	Undisputed Truth
16.	One Bad Apple	Osmonds
17.	Have You Seen Her	Chi-Lites
18.	Want Ads	Honey Cone
19.	Family Affair	Sly & the Family Stone
20.	Spanish Harlem	Aretha Franklin
21.	Draggin' The Line	Tommy James
22.	Riders On The Storm	Doors
23.	Never Can Say Goodbye	Jackson 5
24.	Signs	Five Man Electrical Band
25.	Do You Know What I Mean	Lee Michaels
26.	Sweet & Innocent	Donny Osmond
27.	Gypsys, Tramps & Thieves	Cher
28.	Me & Bobby McGee	Janis Joplin
29.	You've Got A Friend	James Taylor

30.	Lonely Days	Bee Gees
31.	Imagine	John Lennon
32.	Sunshine	Jonathan Edwards
33.	Ain't No Sunshine	Bill Withers
34.	Take Me Home, Country Roads	John Denver
35.	Night They Drove Old Dixie Down	Joan Baez
36.	Born To Wander	Rare Earth
37.	Rainy Days & Mondays	Carpenters
38.	Sweet City Woman	Stampeders
39.	Baby I'm-A Want You	Bread
40.	Love The One You're With	Stephen Stills

Top Hits of 1972:

1.	American Pie	Don McLean
2.	First Time Ever I Saw Your Face	Roberta Flack
3.	Alone Again (Naturally)	Gilbert O'Sullivan
4.	Brandy (You're A Fine Girl)	Looking Glass
5.	Song Sung Blue	Neil Diamond
6.	Baby, Don't Get Hooked On Me	Mac Davis
7.	I Can See Clearly Now	Johnny Nash
8.	I Am Woman	Helen Reddy
9.	Without You	Nilsson
10.	Lean On Me	Bill Withers
11.	Oh Girl	Chi-Lites
12.	Me & Mrs. Jones	Billy Paul
13.	Horse With No Name	America
14.	Nights In White Satin	Moody Blues
15.	Hurting Each Other	Carpenters
16.	Heart Of Gold	Neil Young
17.	I'll Take You There	Staple Singers
18.	Nice To Be With You	Gallery
19.	Everybody Plays The Fool	Main Ingredient
20.	Papa Was A Rolling Stone	Temptations
21.	Ben	Michael Jackson
22.	Black & White	Three Dog Night
23.	Let's Stay Together	Al Green
24.	Too Late To Turn Back Now	
		Cornelius Brothers & Sister Rose
25.	Down By The Lazy River	Osmonds
26.	Clair	Gilbert O'Sullivan
27.	Outa-Space	Billy Preston
28.	Mother & Child Reunion	Paul Simon

29. Back Stabbers   O'Jays
30. Garden Party   Rick Nelson
31. Day After Day   Badfinger
32. Burning Love   Elvis Presley
33. Long Cool Woman (In A Black Dress)   Hollies
34. Sylvia's Mother   Dr. Hook & the Medicine Show
35. Day Dreaming   Aretha Franklin
36. Candy Man   Sammy Davis, Jr.
37. Baby Blue   Badfinger
38. Back Off Boogaloo   Ringo Starr
39. Rockin' Robin   Michael Jackson
40. Precious & Few   Climax

Top Hits of 1973:

1. Heartbeat—It's A Lovebeat — DeFranco Family
2. My Love — Paul McCartney
3. Crocodile Rock — Elton John
4. You're So Vain — Carly Simon
5. Killing Me Softly With His Song — Roberta Flack
6. Tie A Yellow Ribbon Round The Ole Oak Tree — Tony Orlando & Dawn
7. Night The Lights Went Out In Georgia — Vicki Lawrence
8. Half-Breed — Cher
9. Let's Get It On — Marvin Gaye
10. Photograph — Ringo Starr
11. Touch Me In The Morning — Diana Ross
12. Brother Louie — Stories
13. I Got A Name — Jim Croce
14. Hello, It's Me — Todd Rundgren
15. Goodbye Yellow Brick Road — Elton John
16. The Joker — Steve Miller Band
17. Live & Let Die — Paul McCartney & Wings
18. We're An American Band — Grand Funk
19. Loves Me Like A Rock — Paul Simon
20. Superstition — Stevie Wonder
21. Shambala — Three Dog Night
22. Bad, Bad Leroy Brown — Jim Croce
23. Love Train — O'Jays
24. Frankenstein — Edgar Winter Group
25. Will It Go Round In Circles — Billy Preston
26. Also Sprach Zarathustra (2001) — Deodato
27. You Are The Sunshine Of My Life — Stevie Wonder
28. Dueling Banjos — Weissberg & Mandell

29.	The Morning After	Maureen McGovern
30.	Ain't No Woman (Like The One I've Got)	Four Tops
31.	Pillow Talk	Sylvia
32.	Boogie Woogie Bugle Boy	Bette Midler
33.	Cisco Kid	War
34.	Top Of The World	Carpenters
35.	Just You 'N' Me	Chicago
36.	Show & Tell	Al Wilson
37.	Angie	Rolling Stones
38.	Basketball Jones	Cheech & Chong
39.	Get Down	Gilbert O'Sullivan
40.	Long Train Runnin'	Doobie Brothers

Top Hits of 1974:

1.	Seasons In The Sun	Terry Jacks
2.	One Tin Soldier	Coven
3.	The Night Chicago Died	Paper Lace
4.	Rock The Boat	Hues Corporation
5.	I Honestly Love You	Olivia Newton-John
6.	Bennie & The Jets	Elton John
7.	The Streak	Ray Stevens
8.	Kung Fu Fighting	Carl Douglas
9.	You Ain't Seen Nothing Yet	Bachman-Turner Overdrive
10.	The Bitch Is Back	Elton John
11.	Hooked On A Feeling	Blue Swede
12.	Band On The Run	Wings
13.	Loco-Motion	Grand Funk
14.	(You're) Having My Baby	Paul Anka
15.	Life Is A Rock (But The Radio Rolled Me)	Reunion
16.	The Most Beautiful Girl	Charlie Rich
17.	Cat's In The Cradle	Harry Chapin
18.	When Will I See You Again	Three Degrees
19.	Beach Baby	First Class
20.	Billy, Don't Be A Hero	Bo Donaldson & the Heywoods
21.	Sundown	Gordon Lightfoot
22.	Last Kiss	Wednesday
23.	Rock Me Gently	Andy Kim
24.	Rock On	David Essex
25.	Earache My Eye	Cheech & Chong
26.	Rock Your Baby	George McCrae
27.	Annie's Song	John Denver
28.	The Way We Were	Barbra Streisand
29.	Smokin' In The Boy's Room	Brownsville Station

30.	You're 16	Ringo Starr
31.	My Melody Of Love	Bobby Vinton
32.	Come & Get Your Love	Redbone
33.	The Air That I Breathe	Hollies
34.	Takin' Care Of Business	Bachman-Turner Overdrive
35.	I Shot The Sheriff	Eric Clapton
36.	Tell Me Something Good	Rufus
37.	The Lord's Prayer	Sister Janet Mead
38.	Jazzman	Carole King
39.	The Entertainer	Marvin Hamlisch
40.	Dark Lady	Cher

Top Hits of 1975:

1. Love Will Keep Us Together — Captain & Tennille
2. Convoy — C.W. McCall
3. Philadelphia Freedom — Elton John Band
4. Have You Never Been Mellow — Olivia Newton-John
5. Mandy — Barry Manilow
6. Bad Blood — Neil Sedaka
7. Killer Queen — Queen
8. Black Water — Doobie Brothers
9. Get Down Tonight — KC & the Sunshine Band
10. Island Girl — Elton John
11. Someone Saved My Life Tonight — Elton John
12. Listen To What The Man Said — Wings
13. Jackie Blue — Ozark Mountain Daredevils
14. Lucy In The Sky With Diamonds — Elton John
15. Fallin' In Love — Hamilton, Joe Frank & Reynolds
16. Mr. Jaws — Dickie Goodman
17. Saturday Night — Bay City Rollers
18. That's The Way (I Like It) — KC & the Sunshine Band
19. Rhinestone Cowboy — Glen Campbell
20. Sister Golden Hair — America
21. Feelings — Morris Albert
22. Please Mr. Postman — Carpenters
23. Wildfire — Michael Murphey
24. It's A Miracle — Barry Manilow
25. Lady Marmalade — Labelle
26. Lady — Styx
27. Jive Talkin' — Bee Gees
28. Magic — Pilot
29. My Eyes Adored You — Frankie Valli

30. Laughter In The Rain   Neil Sedaka
31. Ballroom Blitz   Sweet
32. No No Song   Ringo Starr
33. Another Somebody Done Somebody Wrong Song

B.J. Thomas
34. Long Tall Glasses (I Can Dance)   Leo Sayer
35. The Way I Want To Touch You   Captain & Tennille
36. Who Loves You   Four Seasons
37. I'm Not In Love   10cc
38. Run Joey Run   David Geddes
39. Lovin' You   Minnie Riperton
40. Dance With Me   Orleans

Top Hits of 1976:

1.	Disco Duck	Rick Dees
2.	Bohemian Rhapsody	Queen
3.	Tonight's The Night	Rod Stewart
4.	Don't Go Breaking My Heart	Elton John & Kiki Dee
5.	Silly Love Songs	Wings
6.	Lonely Night (Angel Face)	Captain & Tennille
7.	If You Leave Me Now	Chicago
8.	50 Ways To Leave Your Lover	Paul Simon
9.	Got To Get You Into My Life	Beatles
10.	Welcome Back	John Sebastian
11.	December, 1963 (Oh, What A Night)	Four Seasons
12.	Afternoon Delight	Starland Vocal Band
13.	Shop Around	Captain & Tennille
14.	I Write The Songs	Barry Manilow
15.	Nadia's Theme	DeVorzon & Botkin, Jr.
16.	Muskrat Love	Captain & Tennille
17.	Devil Woman	Cliff Richard
18.	Play That Funky Music	Wild Cherry
19.	Fox On The Run	Sweet
20.	I Only Want To Be With You	Bay City Rollers
21.	Boogie Fever	Sylvers
22.	Rock & Roll Music	Beach Boys
23.	Dream On	Aerosmith
24.	Shannon	Henry Gross
25.	Let 'Em In	Wings
26.	You Make Me Feel Like Dancing	Leo Sayer
27.	More Than A Feeling	Boston
28.	Get Closer	Seals & Crofts
29.	Get Up & Boogie	Silver Convention

30.	Love Hangover	Diana Ross
31.	The Boys Are Back In Town	Thin Lizzy
32.	You Are The Woman	Firefall
33.	Right Back Where we Started From	Maxine Nightingale
34.	Rock'n Me	Steve Miller
35.	Beth	Kiss
36.	Wreck Of The Edmund Fitzgerald	Gordon Lightfoot
37.	Theme From S.W.A.T.	Rhythm Heritage
38.	Breaking Up Is Hard To Do	Neil Sedaka
39.	I'd Really Love To See You Tonight	England Dan & John Ford Coley
40.	Crazy On You	Heart

Top Hits of 1977:

1.	You Light Up My Life	Debby Boone
2.	I Just Want To Be Your Everything	Andy Gibb
3.	Undercover Angel	Alan O'Day
4.	Da Doo Ron Ron	Shaun Cassidy
5.	Blinded By The Light	Manfred Mann's Earth Band
6.	Torn Between Two Lovers	Mary MacGregor
7.	How Deep Is Your Love	Bee Gees
8.	Hot Line	Sylvers
9.	Boogie Nights	Heatwave
10.	Things We Do For Love	10cc
11.	Rich Girl	Hall & Oates
12.	Weekend In New England	Barry Manilow
13.	When I Need You	Leo Sayer
14.	Southern Nights	Glen Campbell
15.	Sir Duke	Stevie Wonder
16.	Best Of My Love	Emotions
17.	That's Rock 'N' Roll	Shaun Cassidy
18.	Don't It Make My Brown Eyes Blue	Crystal Gayle
19.	Love Theme From "A Star Is Born" (Evergreen)	Barbra Streisand
20.	Dancing Queen	ABBA
21.	Gonna Fly Now	Bill Conti
22.	Star Wars Theme/Cantina Band	Meco
23.	(Your Love Has Lifted Me) Higher & Higher	Rita Coolidge
24.	Lonely Boy	Andrew Gold
25.	Fly Like An Eagle	Steve Miller
26.	Don't Give Up On Us	David Soul
27.	Black Betty	Ram Jam
28.	I'm Your Boogie Man	KC & the Sunshine Band

29.	Carry On Wayward Son	Kansas
30.	Keep It Comin' Love	KC & the Sunshine Band
31.	Lido Shuffle	Boz Scaggs
32.	New Kid In Town	Eagles
33.	You Made Me Believe In Magic	Bay City Rollers
34.	Year Of The Cat	Al Stewart
35.	I'm In You	Peter Frampton
36.	Come Sail Away	Styx
37.	Nobody Does It Better	Carly Simon
38.	Stand Tall	Burton Cummings
39.	Car Wash	Rose Royce
40.	Feels Like The First Time	Foreigner

Top Hits of 1978:

1.	Stayin' Alive	Bee Gees
2.	Le Freak	Chic
3.	Shadow Dancing	Andy Gibb
4.	Kiss You All Over	Exile
5.	Boogie Oogie Oogie	Taste Of Honey
6.	Hot Child In The City	Nick Gilder
7.	We Are The Champions/We Will Rock You	Queen
8.	King Tut	Steve Martin
9.	Night Fever	Bee Gees
10.	Emotion	Samantha Sang
11.	Three Times A Lady	Commodores
12.	Miss You	Rolling Stones
13.	Too Much, Too Little, Too Late	
	Johnny Mathis & Deniece Williams	
14.	You Don't Bring Me Flowers	Barbra & Neil
15.	Runaround Sue	Leif Garrett
16.	You're The One That I Want	
	John Travolta & Olivia Newton-John	
17.	(Love Is) Thicker Than Water	Andy Gibb
18.	Short People	Randy Newman
19.	Just The Way You Are	Billy Joel
20.	MacArthur Park	Donna Summer
21.	Macho Man	Village People
22.	Grease	Frankie Valli
23.	Here You Come Again	Dolly Parton
24.	Hot Blooded	Foreigner
25.	Jack & Jill	Raydio
26.	Flash Light	Parliament
27.	You're In My Heart	Rod Stewart

28.	Last Dance	Donna Summer
29.	Baby Come Back	Player
30.	Baker Street	Gerry Rafferty
31.	Heaven On The 7th Floor	Paul Nicholas
32.	You Needed Me	Anne Murray
33.	Can't Smile Without You	Barry Manilow
34.	With A Little Luck	Wings
35.	Feels So Good	Chuck Mangione
36.	It's A Heartache	Bonnie Tyler
37.	Groove Line	Heatwave
38.	Get Off	Foxy
39.	Dust In The Wind	Kansas
40.	Closer I Get To You	Roberta Flack & Donny Hathaway

Top Hits of 1979:

1. My Sharona — Knack
2. Babe — Styx
3. Hot Stuff — Donna Summer
4. Da Ya Think I'm Sexy — Rod Stewart
5. I Will Survive — Gloria Gaynor
6. Rise — Herb Alpert
7. Reunited — Peaches & Herb
8. Knock On Wood — Amii Stewart
9. Ring My Bell — Anita Ward
10. Bad Girls — Donna Summer
11. Y.M.C.A. — Village People
12. Sad Eyes — Robert John
13. No More Tears (Enough Is Enough) — Barbra Streisand & Donna Summer
14. Good Times — Chic
15. Lovin', Touchin', Squeezin' — Journey
16. What A Fool Believes — Doobie Brothers
17. Fire — Pointer Sisters
18. Heart Of Glass — Blondie
19. Makin' It — David Naughton
20. I Want You To Want Me — Cheap Trick
21. The Devil Went Down To Georgia — Charlie Daniels Band
22. Music Box Dancer — Frank Mills
23. My Life — Billy Joel
24. Too Much Heaven — Bee Gees
25. Pop Muzik — M
26. September — Earth, Wind & Fire
27. Main Event/Fight — Barbra Streisand
28. Shake Your Groove Thing — Peaches & Herb

29.	Shake Your Body (Down To The Ground)	Jacksons
30.	We Don't Talk Anymore	Cliff Richard
31.	Heartache Tonight	Eagles
32.	Tragedy	Bee Gees
33.	Let's Go	Cars
34.	Don't Bring Me Down	Electric Light Orchestra
35.	Sail On	Commodores
36.	Still	Commodores
37.	Do You Think I'm Disco	Steve Dahl
38.	I'll Never Love This Way Again	Dionne Warwick
39.	We Are Family	Sister Sledge
40.	Logical Song	Supertramp

TOP 40 SONGS OF THE 1970S:

1. My Sharona — Knack
2. Stayin' Alive — Bee Gees
3. Le Freak — Chic
4. You Light Up My Life — Debby Boone
5. Babe — Styx
6. Shadow Dancing — Andy Gibb
7. American Pie — Don McLean
8. Joy To The World — Three Dog Night
9. First Time Ever I Saw Your Face — Roberta Flack
10. Kiss You All Over — Exile
11. Love Will Keep Us Together — Captain & Tennille
12. I Just Want To Be Your Everything — Andy Gibb
13. Hot Stuff — Donna Summer
14. Disco Duck — Rick Dees
15. Da Ya Think I'm Sexy — Rod Stewart
16. Convoy — C.W. McCall
17. Bohemian Rhapsody — Queen
18. Tonight's The Night — Rod Stewart
19. Seasons In The Sun — Terry Jacks
20. Don't Go Breaking My Heart — Elton John & Kiki Dee
21. Heartbeat—It's a Lovebeat — DeFranco Family
22. It's Too Late/I Feel The Earth Move — Carole King
23. My Love — Paul McCartney
24. Boogie Oogie Oogie — Taste Of Honey
25. I Will Survive — Gloria Gaynor
26. Hot Child In The City — Nick Gilder
27. We Are The Champions/We Will Rock You — Queen
28. Rise — Herb Alpert
29. Undercover Angel — Alan O'Day

30.	Philadelphia Freedom	Elton John Band
31.	Da Doo Ron Ron	Shaun Cassidy
32.	Silly Love Songs	Wings
33.	Have You Never Been Mellow	Olivia Newton-John
34.	King Tut	Steve Martin
35.	Reunited	Peaches & Herb
36.	Blinded By The Light	Manfred Mann's Earth Band
37.	Mandy	Barry Manilow
38.	One Tin Soldier	Coven
39.	The Night Chicago Died	Paper Lace
40.	Rock The Boat	Hues Corporation

Big 89 Artists of the 1970s

1. Elton John
2. Neil Diamond
3. Bee Gees
4. Paul McCartney
5. Chicago
6. Carpenters
7. Stevie Wonder
8. Three Dog Night
9. Jackson 5
10. Barry Manilow
11. Olivia Newton-John
12. Donny Osmond
13. Eagles
14. Bread
15. Tony Orlando & Dawn
16. Elvis Presley
17. Guess Who
18. Donna Summer
19. Creedence Clearwater Revival
20. Electric Light Orchestra
21. Captain & Tennille
22. Helen Reddy
23. John Denver
24. Rolling Stones
25. Doobie Brothers
26. Diana Ross
27. Rod Stewart
28. War
29. Fifth Dimension

30. B.J. Thomas
31. Al Green
32. Osmonds
33. Linda Ronstadt
34. Carly Simon
35. Queen
36. Fleetwood Mac
37. James Taylor
38. Gladys Knight & the Pips
39. Marvin Gaye
40. Barbra Streisand
41. Styx
42. Cat Stevens
43. Bay City Rollers
44. Cher
45. Ringo Starr
46. Aretha Franklin
47. KC & the Sunshine Band
48. America
49. Stylistics
50. George Harrison
51. ABBA
52. Supremes
53. Glen Campbell
54. Carole King
55. Tom Jones
56. Michael Jackson
57. Paul Simon
58. Spinners
59. Foreigner
60. Steve Miller
61. Anne Murray

62. Temptations
63. Jim Croce
64. Beatles
65. Partridge Family
66. Earth, Wind & Fire
67. Grand Funk
68. Commodores
69. Roberta Flack
70. Kiss
71. Neil Sedaka
72. Lobo
73. Who
74. Four Tops
75. Alice Cooper
76. Andy Gibb
77. John Lennon
78. Grass Roots
79. O'Jays
80. Rare Earth
81. Peter Frampton
82. Led Zeppelin
83. Gilbert O'Sullivan
84. Seals & Crofts
85. Little River Band
86. Leo Sayer
87. Barry White
88. Moody Blues
89. Heart

About the Author

Ron Smith is a 30-year veteran of oldies radio as a disk jockey, program and music director. He served for more than eight years as Music Director of WJMK-FM, Oldies 104.3 in Chicago and was Senior Music Programmer of Internet Radio for RadioWave.com in the Windy City. Since 1995, he has delighted fans of 50s, 60s and 70s music with the Internet's premiere oldies Web site— www.oldiesmusic.com.

He is also the author of *Chicago Top 40 Charts 1960-1969*. He resides in suburban Chicago with his vast music and book libraries.

CPSIA information can be obtained
at www.ICGtesting.com
Printed in the USA
LVHW100714040922
727575LV00019B/153